The USES of the UNIVERSITY

Third Edition

CLARK KERR

Harvard University Press
Cambridge, Massachusetts
London, England

The Godkin Lectures on the Essentials of
Free Government and the Duties of the Citizen
were established at Harvard University in 1903
in memory of Edwin Lawrence Godkin (1831–1902).
They are given annually under the auspices of the
Harvard Graduate School of Public Administration,
which in 1966 was renamed the John F. Kennedy
School of Government.

10 9 8 7 6 5 4 3

Library of Congress Cataloging in Publication Data

Kerr, Clark, 1911–
    The uses of the university.

    "Based on the 1963 Godkin lectures, delivered at
Harvard University on April 23, 24, and 25, 1963"—Pref.,
1963.
    Originally published: The uses of the university,
with a "Postscript—1972." Cambridge, Mass.: Harvard
University Press, 1972. (The Godkin lectures at Harvard
University; 1963) With new pref. and a "Postscript—
1982."
    Includes bibliographical references and index.
    1. Education, Higher—Addresses, essays, lectures.
I. Title.   II. Series: Godkin lectures; 1963.
LB 2325.K43 1982   378   82-3146
ISBN 0-674-93171-8   AACR2

PREFACE, 1982

"Postscript—1972" was concerned with "how I wish I had written these lectures *in 1963*." A small, and too often rather nondescript, literature had by that time grown up around *The Uses of the University,* some of it based upon careless misunderstandings and some of it on deliberate misinterpretations. I wanted to set the record straight, as I saw it, and indulge in some painful reconsiderations of my own.

"Postscript—1982" has a quite separate purpose. In 1972, I asked the urgent questions: "whether or not a slow exit is what is now happening to the American model" of the university; whether "1870 to 1970" will "have been the century of the rise and the beginning of the decline of the American university"; or, whether, "after a pause for a time of troubles, it will gain new strength and rise to ever greater heights." But I set these questions aside unanswered.

Many answers, in an orgy of hate and despair, were then being given—mostly that higher education generally and the university specifically were fated to decline. In the fall of 1973 I spoke at the annual meeting of the American Council on Education on "The Moods of Academia."[1] I noted some of the recently published books that stared out at me from my shelves with titles or subtitles like these:

Academia in Anarchy (1970)
Academics in Retreat (1971)
Academy in Turmoil (1971)
American Universities in Crisis (1968)
Anarchy in the Groves of Academe (1970)

Back to the Middle Ages (1969)
Bankruptcy of Academic Policy (1972)
Blow It Up (1971)
Blind Man on a Freeway (1971)

Chaos in Our Colleges (1963)
Confrontation and Counter-Attack (1971)

Death of the American University (1973)
Destruction of a College President (1972)
Degradation of the Academic Dogma (1971)
Down and Out in Academia (1972)

Embattled University (1970)
Exploding University (1971)

Fall of the American University (1972)

This was only a sample, and the list could have been continued down through the alphabet. I said that "this is what some of our 'best' and our 'brightest' in higher education—defined as those who get books published—think about us." It still seems strange to me that persons with such highly trained intellects should also be such chameleons of mood when their own interests seem threatened—more reactive to current events than reflective of historical perspective.

But were these views correct? I answered: "To those who see only gloom and doom, we can say that much that is good is occurring. To those who say that everything fails, we can say that much is, in fact, succeeding. To those who see only problems, we can say there are possibilities available for their alleviation." I was speaking then as Chairman of the Carnegie Commission on Higher Education engaged in what became in total a twelve-year survey of and recommendation about American higher education. The subsequent Carnegie Council on Policy Studies in Higher Education, which I also chaired, concluded in its final report in 1980 that, actually, in retrospect, "the 1970s . . . was a good decade for higher education."[2]

Seldom have the fears of some academics at the time and the realities of history in retrospect been so far apart.

What have we learned about the American university out of the 1970's that started out with such despair but ended up as a "good decade" and out of the turbulent 1960's? Certainly we have learned to treat with caution the overblown rhetoric and defective current judgments of many of our scholars studying higher education when they are under stress. Too many of them were themselves blind men on a freeway, not knowing which way the traffic was flowing. But what else have we learned? And what may we now expect of the American university in a continuing time of troubles but with new dimensions to those troubles? These are the questions to which "Postscript—1982" is briefly addressed.

CLARK KERR

President Emeritus,

University of California

Berkeley, California
March, 1982

PREFACE, 1963

Universities in America are at a hinge of history: while connected with their past, they are swinging in another direction. This volume, based on the 1963 Godkin Lectures, delivered at Harvard University on April 23, 24, and 25, 1963, attempts to describe and to evaluate some of the significant new developments in American higher education. The title, "The Uses of the University," implies a generally optimistic tone, for it is not the *misuses* of the university that will mainly concern us. At the same time, however, it is well to note that in the discussion that follows, analysis should not be confused with approval or description with defense.

Although it is one of our oldest social institutions, the university today finds itself in a quite novel position in society. It faces its new role with few precedents to fall back on, with little but platitudes to mask the nakedness of the change. Instead of platitudes and nostalgic glances backward to what it once was, the university needs a rigorous look at the reality of the world it occupies today.

The basic reality, for the university, is the wide-

vii

spread recognition that new knowledge is the most important factor in economic and social growth. We are just now perceiving that the university's invisible product, knowledge, may be the most powerful single element in our culture, affecting the rise and fall of professions and even of social classes, of regions and even of nations.

Because of this fundamental reality, the university is being called upon to produce knowledge as never before—for civic and regional purposes, for national purposes, and even for no purpose at all beyond the realization that most knowledge eventually comes to serve mankind. And it is also being called upon to transmit knowledge to an unprecedented proportion of the population.

This reality is reshaping the very nature and quality of the university. Old concepts of faculty-student relations, of research, of faculty-administration roles are being changed at a rate without parallel. And this at a time when it seems that an entire generation is pounding at the gates and demanding admission. To the academician, conservative by nature, the sound made by the new generation often resembles the howl of a mob. To the politician, it is a signal to be obeyed. To the administrator, it is a warning that we are in new times and that the decisions we make now will be uncommonly productive—both of good and ill.

Thus the university has come to have a new centrality for all of us, as much for those who never see the ivied halls as for those who pass through them or reside there.

The university has been a remarkably unstudied institution until very recently. Seymour Harris was one of the first of my fellow economists to examine education as one might any other activity of society and to subject it to economic analysis. Today education, including higher education, is being scrutinized in all its aspects. This reflects the increasing recognition of its uses in economic growth, in international competition, in political and social as well as cultural development. One can only wonder whether the university was a better place before people began writing and talking so much about it—before they became so conscious of its uses.

CLARK KERR

Berkeley, California

A FURTHER WORD

In view of the continuing ferment in our universities since 1963, the publisher has suggested that I write an additional chapter in which I would look again at the original text and the discussion it has occasioned. I am pleased to comply. The new chapter, entitled "Postscript—1972," begins on page 127. The earlier chapters remain as they were.

CLARK KERR
Chairman, Carnegie Commission
on Higher Education

Berkeley, California
April 3, 1972

CONTENTS

I

THE IDEA OF
A MULTIVERSITY

THE university started as a single community—a community of masters and students. It may even be said to have had a soul in the sense of a central animating principle. Today the large American university is, rather, a whole series of communities and activities held together by a common name, a common governing board, and related purposes. This great transformation is regretted by some, accepted by many, gloried in, as yet, by few. But it should be understood by all.

The university of today can perhaps be understood, in part, by comparing it with what it once was—with the academic cloister of Cardinal Newman, with the research organism of Abraham Flexner. Those are the ideal types from which it has derived, ideal types which still constitute the illusions of some of its inhabitants. The modern American university, however, is not Oxford nor is it

Berlin; it is a new type of institution in the world. As a new type of institution, it is not really private and it is not really public; it is neither entirely of the world nor entirely apart from it. It is unique.

"The Idea of a University" was, perhaps, never so well expressed as by Cardinal Newman when engaged in founding the University of Dublin a little over a century ago.[1] His views reflected the Oxford of his day whence he had come. A university, wrote Cardinal Newman, is "the high protecting power of all knowledge and science, of fact and principle, of inquiry and discovery, of experiment and speculation; it maps out the territory of the intellect, and sees that . . . there is neither encroachment nor surrender on any side." He favored "liberal knowledge," and said that "useful knowledge" was a "deal of trash."

Newman was particularly fighting the ghost of Bacon who some 250 years before had condemned "a kind of adoration of the mind . . . by means whereof men have withdrawn themselves too much from the contemplation of nature, and the observations of experience, and have tumbled up and down in their own reason and conceits." Bacon believed that knowledge should be for the benefit and use of men, that it should "not be as a courtesan, for pleasure and vanity only, or as a bond-woman, to acquire and gain to her master's use; but as a spouse, for generation, fruit and comfort."[2]

To this Newman replied that "Knowledge is

capable of being its own end. Such is the constitution of the human mind, that any kind of knowledge, if it really be such, is its own reward." And in a sharp jab at Bacon he said: "The Philosophy of Utility, you will say, Gentlemen, has at least done its work; and I grant it—it aimed low, but it has fulfilled its aim." Newman felt that other institutions should carry on research, for "If its object were scientific and philosophical discovery, I do not see why a University should have any students"—an observation sardonically echoed by today's students who often think their professors are not interested in them at all but only in research. A University training, said Newman, "aims at raising the intellectual tone of society, at cultivating the public mind, at purifying the national taste, at supplying true principles to popular enthusiasm and fixed aims to popular aspirations, at giving enlargement and sobriety to the ideas of the age, at facilitating the exercise of political powers, and refining the intercourse of private life." It prepares a man "to fill any post with credit, and to master any subject with facility."

This beautiful world was being shattered forever even as it was being so beautifully portrayed. By 1852, when Newman wrote, the German universities were becoming the new model. The democratic and industrial and scientific revolutions were all well underway in the western world. The gentleman "at home in any society" was soon to be at home in none. Science was beginning to take the place of moral philosophy, research the place of teaching.

"The Idea of a Modern University," to use Flexner's phrase,[3] was already being born. "A University," said Flexner in 1930, "is not outside, but inside the general social fabric of a given era. . . . It is not something apart, something historic, something that yields as little as possible to forces and influences that are more or less new. It is on the contrary . . . an expression of the age, as well as an influence operating upon both present and future."

It was clear by 1930 that "Universities have changed profoundly—and commonly in the direction of the social evolution of which they are part." This evolution had brought departments into universities, and still new departments; institutes and ever more institutes; created vast research libraries; turned the philosopher on his log into a researcher in his laboratory or the library stacks; taken medicine out of the hands of the profession and put it into the hands of the scientists; and much more. Instead of the individual student, there were the needs of society; instead of Newman's eternal "truths in the natural order," there was discovery of the new; instead of the generalist, there was the specialist. The university became, in the words of Flexner, "an institution consciously devoted to the pursuit of knowledge, the solution of problems, the critical appreciation of achievement and the training of men at a really high level." No longer could a single individual "master any subject"—Newman's universal liberal man was gone forever.

But as Flexner was writing of the "Modern University," it, in turn, was ceasing to exist. The Berlin of Humboldt was being violated just as Berlin had violated the soul of Oxford. The universities were becoming too many things. Flexner himself complained that they were "secondary schools, vocational schools, teacher-training schools, research centers, 'uplift' agencies, businesses—these and other things simultaneously." They engaged in "incredible absurdities," "a host of inconsequential things." They "needlessly cheapened, vulgarized and mechanized themselves." Worst of all, they became " 'service stations' for the general public."

Even Harvard. "It is clear," calculated Flexner, "that of Harvard's total expenditures not more than one-eighth is devoted to the *central* university disciplines at the level at which a university ought to be conducted." He wondered: "Who has forced Harvard into this false path? No one. It does as it pleases; and this sort of thing pleases." It obviously did not please Flexner. He wanted Harvard to disown the Graduate School of Business and let it become, if it had to survive it all, the "Boston School of Business." He would also have banished all Schools of Journalism and Home Economics, football, correspondence courses, and much else.

It was not only Harvard and other American universities, but also London. Flexner asked "in what

sense the University of London is a university at all."
It was only "a federation."

By 1930, American universities had moved a long
way from Flexner's "Modern University" where
"The heart of a university is a graduate school of
arts and sciences, the solidly professional schools
(mainly, in America, medicine and law) and certain
research institutes." They were becoming less and
less like a "genuine university," by which Flexner
meant "an organism, characterized by highness and
definiteness of aim, unity of spirit and purpose." The
"Modern University" was as nearly dead in 1930
when Flexner wrote about it as the old Oxford was
in 1852 when Newman idealized it. History moves
faster than the observer's pen. Neither the ancient
classics and theology nor the German philosophers
and scientists could set the tone for the really modern
university—the multiversity.

"The Idea of a Multiversity" has no bard to sing
its praises; no prophet to proclaim its vision; no
guardian to protect its sanctity. It has its critics, its
detractors, its transgressors. It also has its barkers
selling its wares to all who will listen—and many
do. But it also has its reality rooted in the logic of
history. It is an imperative rather than a reasoned
choice among elegant alternatives.

President Nathan Pusey wrote in his latest annual
report to the members of the Harvard Board of
Overseers that the average date of graduation of the
present Board members was 1924; and much has

happened to Harvard since 1924. Half of the buildings are new. The faculty has grown five-fold, the budget nearly fifteen-fold. "One can find almost anywhere one looks similar examples of the effect wrought in the curriculum and in the nature of the contemporary university by widening international awareness, advancing knowledge, and increasingly sophisticated methods of research. . . . Asia and Africa, radio telescopes, masers and lasers and devices for interplanetary exploration unimagined in 1924—these and other developments have effected such enormous changes in the intellectual orientation and aspiration of the contemporary university as to have made the university we knew as students now seem a strangely underdeveloped, indeed a very simple and an almost unconcerned kind of institution. And the pace of change continues."[4]

Not only at Harvard. The University of California last year had operating expenditures from all sources of nearly half a billion dollars, with almost another 100 million for construction; a total employment of over 40,000 people, more than IBM and in a far greater variety of endeavors; operations in over a hundred locations, counting campuses, experiment stations, agricultural and urban extension centers, and projects abroad involving more than fifty countries; nearly 10,000 courses in its catalogues; some form of contact with nearly every industry, nearly every level of government, nearly every person in its region. Vast amounts of expensive equipment were serviced and maintained. Over 4,000 babies were born in its hospitals. It is the world's largest purveyor of white mice. It will soon have the world's largest primate colony. It will soon also have 100,000 students—30,000 of them at the graduate level; yet much less than one third of its expenditures are directly related to teaching. It already has nearly 200,000 students in extension courses—including one out of every three lawyers and one out of every six doctors in the state. And Harvard and California are illustrative of many more.

Newman's "Idea of a University" still has its devotees—chiefly the humanists and the generalists and the undergraduates. Flexner's "Idea of a Modern University" still has its supporters—chiefly the scientists and the specialists and the graduate students. "The Idea of a Multiversity" has its practitioners—chiefly the administrators, who now number many of the faculty among them, and the leadership groups in society at large. The controversies are still around in the faculty clubs and the student coffee houses; and the models of Oxford and Berlin and modern Harvard all animate segments of what was once a "community of masters and students" with a single vision of its nature and purpose. These several competing visions of true purpose, each relating to a different layer of history, a different web of forces, cause much of the malaise in the university communities of today. The university is so many things to so many different people that it must, of necessity, be partially at war with itself.

How did the multiversity happen? No man created it; in fact, no man visualized it. It has been a long time coming about and it has a long way to go. What is its history? How is it governed? What is life like within it? What is its justification? Does it have a future?

THE STRANDS OF HISTORY

The multiversity draws on many strands of history. To the extent that its origins can be identified, they can be traced to the Greeks. But there were several traditions even then. Plato had his Academy devoted to truth largely for its own sake, but also truth for the philosophers who were to be kings. The Sophists, whom Plato detested so much that he gave them an evil aura persisting to this day, had their schools too. These schools taught rhetoric and other useful skills—they were more interested in attainable success in life than they were in the unattainable truth. The Pythagoreans were concerned, among other things, with mathematics and astronomy. The modern academician likes to trace his intellectual forebears to the groves of Academe; but the modern university with its professional schools and scientific institutes might look equally to the Sophists and the Pythagoreans. The humanists, the professionals, and the scientists all have their roots in ancient times. The "Two Cultures" or the "Three Cultures" are almost as old as culture itself.

Despite its Greek precursors, however, the university is, as Hastings Rashdall wrote, "a distinctly medieval institution."[5] In the Middle Ages it developed many of the features that prevail today— a name and a central location, masters with a degree of autonomy, students, a system of lectures, a procedure for examinations and degrees, and even an administrative structure with its "faculties." Salerno in medicine, Bologna in law, and Paris in theology and philosophy were the great pacesetters. The university came to be a center for the professions, for the study of the classics, for theological and philosophical disputes. Oxford and Cambridge, growing out of Paris, developed in their distinctive ways with their particular emphasis on the residential college instead of the separate faculties as the primary unit.

By the end of the eighteenth century the European universities had long since become oligarchies, rigid in their subject matter, centers of reaction in their societies—opposed, in large part, to the Reformation, unsympathetic to the spirit of creativity of the Renaissance, antagonistic to the new science. There was something almost splendid in their disdain for contemporary events. They stood like castles without windows, profoundly introverted. But the tides of change can cut very deep. In

France the universities were swept away by the Revolution, as they almost had been in England at the time of Cromwell.

It was in Germany that the rebirth of the university took place. Halle had dropped teaching exclusively in Latin in 1693; Göttingen had started the teaching of history in 1736; but it was the establishment of Berlin by Wilhelm von Humboldt in 1809 from his vantage point in the Prussian Ministry that was the dramatic event. The emphasis was on philosophy and science, on research, on graduate instruction, on the freedom of professors and students (*Lehrfreiheit* and *Lernfreiheit*). The department was created, and the institute. The professor was established as a great figure within and without the university. The Berlin plan spread rapidly throughout Germany, which was then entering a period of industrialization and intense nationalism following the shock of the defeat at the hands of Napoleon. The university carried with it two great new forces: science and nationalism. It is true that the German university system later bogged down through its uncritical reliance on the great professorial figure who ruled for life over his department and institute, and that it could be subverted by Hitler because of its total dependence on the state. But this does not vitiate the fact that the German university in the nineteenth century was one of the vigorous new institutions in the world.

In 1809 when Berlin was founded, the United

States already had a number of colleges developed on the model of the colleges at Oxford and Cambridge. They concentrated on Calvinism for the would-be preacher and classics for the young gentleman. Benjamin Franklin had had other ideas for the University of Pennsylvania, then the College of Philadelphia, in the 1750's.[6] Reflecting Locke, he wanted "a *more useful* culture of young minds." He was interested in training people for agriculture and commerce; in exploring science. Education should "serve mankind." These ideas were not to take root for another century. Drawing on the French Enlightenment, Jefferson started the University of Virginia with a broad curriculum including mathematics and science, and with the electives that Eliot was to make so famous at Harvard half a century later. He put great emphasis on a library—an almost revolutionary idea at the time. Again the application of the ideas was to be long delayed.

The real line of development for the modern American university began with Professor George Ticknor at Harvard in 1825. He tried to reform Harvard on the model of Göttingen where he had studied, and found that reforming Harvard must wait for an Eliot with forty years and the powers of the presidency at his disposal. Yale at the time was the great center of reaction—its famous faculty report of 1828 was a ringing proclamation to do nothing, or at least nothing that had not always been done at Yale or by God.[7] Francis Wayland at Brown in the 1850's made a great fight for the German system, including a program of electives, as did Henry Tappan at Michigan—both without success.

Then the breakthrough came. Daniel Coit Gilman, disenchanted with the then grim prospects at California, became the first president of the new university of Johns Hopkins in 1876. The institution began as a graduate school with an emphasis on research. For Flexner, Gilman was the great hero-figure—and Johns Hopkins "the most stimulating influence that higher education in America had ever known." Charles W. Eliot at Harvard followed the Gilman breakthrough and Harvard during his period (1869 to 1909) placed great emphasis on the graduate school, the professional school, and research—it became a university. But Eliot made his own particular contribution by establishing the elective system permitting students to choose their own courses of study. Others quickly followed—Andrew Dickson White at Cornell, James B. Angell at Michigan, Frederick Barnard at Columbia, William W. Folwell at Minnesota, David Starr Jordan at Stanford, William Rainey Harper at Chicago, Charles K. Adams at Wisconsin, Benjamin Ide Wheeler at California. The state universities, just then expanding, followed the Hopkins idea. Yale and Princeton trailed behind.

The Hopkins idea brought with it the graduate

school with exceptionally high academic standards in what was still a rather new and raw civilization; the renovation of professional education, particularly in medicine; the establishment of the pre-eminent influence of the department; the creation of research institutes and centers, of university presses and learned journals and the "academic ladder"; and also the great proliferation of courses. If students were to be free to choose their courses (one aspect of the *Lernfreiheit* of the early nineteenth-century German university), then professors were free to offer their wares (as *Lehrfreiheit*, the other great slogan of the developing German universities of a century and a half ago, essentially assured). The elective system, however, came more to serve the professors than the students for whom it was first intended, for it meant that the curriculum was no longer controlled by educational policy as the Yale faculty in 1828 had insisted that it should be. Each professor had his own interests, each professor wanted the status of having his own special course, each professor got his own course—and university catalogues came to include 3,000 or more of them. There was, of course, as a result of the new research, more knowledge to spread over the 3,000 courses; otherwise the situation would have been impossible. In any event, freedom for the student to choose became freedom for the professor to invent; and the professor's love of specialization has become the student's hate of fragmentation. A kind of bizarre version of academic laissez-faire has emerged. The student, unlike Adam Smith's idealized buyer, *must* consume—usually at the rate of fifteen hours a week. The modern university was born.

Along with the Hopkins experiment came the land grant movement—and these two influences turned out to be more compatible than might at first appear. The one was Prussian, the other American; one elitist, the other democratic; one academically pure, the other sullied by contact with the soil and the machine. The one looked to Kant and Hegel, the other to Franklin, Jefferson, and Lincoln. But they both served an industrializing nation and they both did it through research and the training of technical competence. Two strands of history were woven together in the modern American university. Michigan became a German-style university and Harvard a land grant type of institution, without the land.

The land grant movement brought schools of agriculture and engineering (in Germany relegated to the *Technische Hochschulen*), of home economics and business administration; opened the doors of universities to the children of farmers and workers, as well as of the middle and upper classes; introduced agricultural experiment stations and service bureaus. Allan Nevins in commenting on the Morrill Act of 1862 said: "The law annexed wide neglected areas to the domain of instruction. Widening the gates of opportunity, it made democracy freer, more adaptable and more kinetic."[8]

A major new departure in the land grant movement came before World War I when the land grant universities extended their activities beyond their campus boundaries. "The Wisconsin Idea" came to flower under the progressivism of the first Roosevelt and the first La Follette. The University of Wisconsin, particularly during the presidency of Charles Van Hise (1903 to 1918), entered the legislative halls in Madison with reform programs, supported the trade union movement through John R. Commons, developed agricultural and urban extension as never before. The university served the whole state. Other state universities did likewise. Even private universities, like Chicago and Columbia, developed important extension programs.

New contacts with the community were created. University athletics became, particularly in the 1920's, a form of public entertainment, which is not unknown even in the 1960's, even in the Ivy League. Once started, university spectator sports could not be killed even by the worst of teams or the best of de-emphasis; and few universities seriously sought after either.

A counterrevolution against these developments was occasionally waged. A. Lawrence Lowell at Harvard (1909 to 1934) emphasized the under-graduate houses and concentration of course work, as against the graduate work and electives of Eliot. It is a commentary not just on Harvard but also on the modern American university that Eliot and Lowell could look in opposite directions and the same institution could follow them both and glory in it. Universities have a unique capacity for riding off in all directions and still staying in the same place, as Harvard has so decisively demonstrated. At Chicago, long after Lowell, Robert M. Hutchins tried to take the university back to Cardinal Newman, to Thomas Aquinas, and to Plato and Aristotle. He succeeded in reviving the philosophic dialogue he loves so well and practices so expertly; but Chicago went on being a modern American university.

Out of the counterreformation, however, came a great new emphasis on student life—particularly undergraduate. Earnest attempts were made to create American counterparts of Oxford and Cambridge; residence halls, student unions, intramural playfields, undergraduate libraries, counseling centers sprang up in many places during the thirties, forties, and fifties. This was a long way from the pure German model, which had provided the student with only the professor and the classroom, and which had led Tappan to abolish dormitories at Michigan. British influence was back, as it was also with the introduction of honors programs, tutorials, independent study.

Out of all these fragments, experiments, and conflicts a kind of unlikely consensus has been reached.

Undergraduate life seeks to follow the British, who have done the best with it, and an historical line that goes back to Plato; the humanists often find their sympathies here. Graduate life and research follow the Germans, who once did best with them, and an historical line that goes back to Pythagoras; the scientists lend their support to all this. The "lesser" professions (lesser than law and medicine) and the service activities follow the American pattern, since the Americans have been best at them, and an historical line that goes back to the Sophists; the social scientists are most likely to be sympathetic. Lowell found his greatest interest in the first, Eliot in the second, and James Bryant Conant (1934 to 1954) in the third line of development and in the synthesis. The resulting combination does not seem plausible but it has given America a remarkably effective educational institution. A university anywhere can aim no higher than to be as British as possible for the sake of the undergraduates, as German as possible for the sake of the graduates and the research personnel, as American as possible for the sake of the public at large—and as confused as possible for the sake of the preservation of the whole uneasy balance.

THE GOVERNANCE OF THE MULTIVERSITY

The multiversity is an inconsistent institution. It is not one community but several—the community of the undergraduate and the community of the graduate; the community of the humanist, the community of the social scientist, and the community of the scientist; the communities of the professional schools; the community of all the nonacademic personnel; the community of the administrators. Its edges are fuzzy—it reaches out to alumni, legislators, farmers, businessmen, who are all related to one or more of these internal communities. As an institution, it looks far into the past and far into the future, and is often at odds with the present. It serves society almost slavishly—a society it also criticizes, sometimes unmercifully. Devoted to equality of opportunity, it is itself a class society. A community, like the medieval communities of masters and students, should have common interests; in the multiversity, they are quite varied, even conflicting. A community should have a soul, a single animating principle; the multiversity has several—some of them quite good, although there is much debate on which souls really deserve salvation.

The multiversity is a name. This means a great deal more than it sounds as though it might. The name of the institution stands for a certain standard of performance, a certain degree of respect, a certain historical legacy, a characteristic quality of spirit. This is of the utmost importance to faculty and to students, to the government agencies and the industries with which the institution deals. Protection and enhancement of the prestige of the name are central to the multiversity. How good is its reputation, what John J. Corson calls its "institutional character"?[9]

Flexner thought of a university as an "organism." In an organism, the parts and the whole are inextricably bound together. Not so the multiversity—many parts can be added and subtracted with little effect on the whole or even little notice taken or any blood spilled. It is more a mechanism—a series of processes producing a series of results—a mechanism held together by administrative rules and powered by money.

Hutchins once described the modern university as a series of separate schools and departments held together by a central heating system. In an area where heating is less important and the automobile more, I have sometimes thought of it as a series of individual faculty entrepreneurs held together by a common grievance over parking.

It is, also, a system of government like a city, or a city state: the city state of the multiversity. It may be inconsistent but it must be governed—not as the guild it once was, but as a complex entity with greatly fractionalized power. There are several competitors for this power.

The students. The students had all the power once; that was in Bologna. Their guilds ran the university and dominated the masters. And the students were tougher on the masters than the masters have ever been on the students. The Bologna pattern had an impact on Salamanca and Spain generally and then in Latin America, where students to this day are usually found in the top governing councils. Their impact is generally more to lower than to raise academic standards although there are exceptions such as Buenos Aires after Peron under the leadership of Risieri Frondizi. Students also involve the university as an institution in the national political controversies of the moment.

Jefferson tried a system of student self-government in the 1820's but quickly abandoned it when all the professors tendered their resignations. He favored self-government by both students and faculty, but never discovered how both could have it at the same time—nor has anybody else. Although José Ortega y Gassett, in addressing the student federation at the University of Madrid, was willing to turn over the entire "mission of the university" to the students, he neglected to comment on faculty reaction.[10]

As part of the "Wisconsin idea" before World War I, there was quite a wave of creation of student governments. They found their power in the area of extracurricular activities, where it has remained. Their extracurricular programs helped broaden student life in such diverse fields as debating, theatrical productions, literary magazines.

Students do have considerable strictly academic influence, however, quite beyond that with which they are usually credited. The system of electives gives them a chance to help determine in which areas and disciplines a university will grow. Their choices, as consumers, guide university expansion and contraction, and this process is far superior to a more rigid guild system of producer determination as in medicine where quotas are traditional. Also students, by their patronage, designate the university teachers. The faculty may, in fact, appoint the faculty, but within this faculty group the students choose the real teachers. In a large university a quarter of the faculty may be selected by the students to do half or more of the actual teaching; the students also "select" ten percent or more to do almost none at all.

The faculty. The guilds of masters organized and ran the University of Paris, and later they did the same at Oxford and Cambridge. Faculty control at Oxford and Cambridge, through the colleges, has remained stronger than anywhere else over the centuries, but even there it has been greatly diminished in recent times.

In the United States, the first great grant of power to the faculty of a major university was at Yale when Jeremiah Day was president (1817 to 1846). It was during the Day regime that the Yale faculty report of 1828 was issued. Harvard has had, by contrast, as McGeorge Bundy has said in his inimitable style, "a tradition of quite high-handed and centralized executive behavior—and it has not suffered, in balance, as a consequence."[11]

Faculties generally in the United States and the

British Commonwealth, some earlier and some later, have achieved authority over admissions, approval of courses, examinations, and granting of degrees— all handled in a rather routine fashion from the point of view of the faculty as a whole. They have also achieved considerable influence over faculty appointments and academic freedom, which are not handled routinely. Faculty control and influence in these areas are essential to the proper conduct of academic life. Once the elective system was established, educational policy became less important to the faculty, although, as at Harvard under Lowell, the elective system was modified to call for general rules on concentration and distribution of work. Since Harvard adopted its program for general education in 1945[12] and Hutchins left Chicago, there has been remarkably little faculty discussion of general educational policy. By contrast, there has been a great deal in England, particularly in the "new universities," where faculty discussion of educational policy has been very lively, and faculty influence, as a consequence, substantial.

Organized faculty control or influence over the general direction of growth of the American multiversity has been quite small, as illustrated by the development of the federal grant university. Individual faculty influence, however, has been quite substantial, even determinative, in the expanding areas of institutes and research grants. Still it is a long way from Paris at the time of Abelard.

Public authority. "Public" authority is a very mixed entity of emperors and popes, ministers of education, grants committees, trustees, and Royal Commissions. But almost everywhere, regardless of the origin of the system, there has come to be a public authority. Even in the Middle Ages, emperors and popes, dukes, cardinals, and city councils came to authorize or establish the universities to make them legitimate—the guild alone was not enough. When Henry VIII had trouble about a wife it shook Oxford and Cambridge to the core.

In modern times, Napoleon was the first to seize control of a university system. He completely reorganized it and made it part of the nationally administered educational system of France, as it remains to this day. He separated off research activities and special training institutions for teachers, engineers, and so forth. The universities became a series of loosely related professional schools. Not until the 1890's were the universities brought back together as meaningful entities and a measure of faculty control restored. Soviet Russia has followed the French pattern with even greater state control.

In Germany, the state governments traditionally have controlled the universities in great detail. So also has the government in Italy. In Latin America a degree of formal autonomy from the government has either been retained or attained, although informal reality usually contradicts the theory.

Even in Great Britain, the "public" has moved in on the faculties. Royal Commissions have helped modernize Oxford and Cambridge. The Redbrick and Scottish universities and London either have had from the beginning or acquired governing boards of a mixed nature, including lay members representative of public authority. Since 1919, and particularly since World War II, the University Grants Committee has made its influence felt in a less and less gentle and more and more effective way.

The lay board has been the distinctive American device for "public" authority in connection with universities, although the device was used in Holland in the late sixteenth century. Beyond the lay board in the state universities are the state department of finance and the governor and the legislature with a tendency toward increasingly detailed review.

Richard Hofstadter has made the interesting observation that the first lay board and the first effective concept of academic freedom developed in Holland at the same time; and that academic freedom has never been inherited from some Golden Age of the past but has instead been imported from the institutions of the surrounding society.[13]

Through all these devices, public influences have been asserted in university affairs. Public influence has increased as much in Paris as student influence has declined in Bologna. Everywhere, with the decreasing exception of Oxford and Cambridge, the ultimate authority lies in the "public" domain; everywhere, with a few exceptions, it is fortunately not exercised in an ultimate fashion. We have, however, come a long way from the guilds of masters, the guilds of students, the guilds of masters and students. The location of power has generally moved from inside to outside the original community of masters and students. The nature of the multiversity makes it inevitable that this historical transfer will not be reversed in any significant fashion, although the multiversity does permit the growth of subcultures which can be relatively autonomous and can have an impact on the totality.

The distribution of power is of great importance. In Germany it came to be lodged too completely in the figure of the full professor at one end and the minister of education at the other; in Oxford and Cambridge, at one time, in an oligarchy of professors; in the United States, during a substantial period, almost exclusively in the president; in Latin America, too often, in the students within and the politicians without.

Influences—external and semi-external. Beyond the formal structure of power, as lodged in students, faculty, administration, or "public" instrumentalities, lie the sources of informal influence. The American system is particularly sensitive to the pressures of its many particular publics. Continental and British universities are less intertwined with their surrounding societies than the American and thus more inward-looking and self-contained. When "the borders of the campus are the boundaries of our state," the lines dividing what is internal from what is external become quite blurred; taking the campus to the state brings the state to the campus. In the so-called "private" universities, alumni, donors, foundations, the federal agencies, the professional and business communities bulk large among the semi-external influences; and in the so-called "public" universities, the agricultural, trade union, and public school communities are likely to be added to the list, and also a more searching press. The multiversity has many "publics" with many interests; and by the very nature of the multiversity many of these interests are quite legitimate and others are quite frivolous.

The administration. The original medieval universities had at the start nothing that could be identified as a separate administration, but one quickly developed. The guild of masters or students selected a rector; and later there were deans of the faculties. At Oxford and Cambridge, there came to be the masters of the colleges. In more modern times in France, Germany, and Italy, the rector has come to stand between the faculty and the minister of education, closer to the minister of education in France and closer to the faculty in Germany; internally he has served principally as chairman of the council of deans where deans still retain substantial authority as in France and Italy. In Germany the full professor, chairman of his department, director of his institute, is a figure of commanding authority.

Even in England, even in Oxford and Cambridge, the central administration is attaining more influence—the vice chancellorship can no longer be rotated casually among the masters. The vice chancellor now must deal with the university grants committee and the vice chancellors of the other universities. The university itself is a much more important unit with its research laboratories, central library, its lecturers in specialized subjects; the college is much less self-contained than it was. All of this has created something of a crisis in the administration of Oxford and Cambridge where administrators once were not to be seen or heard and the work was accomplished by a handful of clerks working in a Dickensian office. Oxbridge is becoming more like the Redbricks. London is *sui generis*.

The general rule is that the administration everywhere becomes, by force of circumstances if not by choice, a more prominent feature of the university. As the institution becomes larger, administration becomes more formalized and separated as a distinct function; as the institution becomes more complex, the role of administration becomes more central in integrating it; as it becomes more related to the once external world, the administration assumes the burdens of these relationships. The managerial revolution has been going on also in the university.

MULTIVERSITY PRESIDENT, GIANT
OR MEDIATOR-INITIATOR?

It is sometimes said that the American multiversity president is a two-faced character. This is not so. If he were, he could not survive. He is a many-faced character, in the sense that he must face in many directions at once while contriving to turn his back on no important group. In this he is different in degree from his counterparts of rectors and vice chancellors, since they face in fewer directions because their institutions have fewer doors and windows to the outside world. The difference, however, is not one of kind. And intensities of relationships vary greatly; the rector of a Latin American university, from this point of view, may well have the most trying task of all, though he is less intertwined in a range of relationships than the North American university president.

The university president in the United States is expected to be a friend of the students, a colleague of the faculty, a good fellow with the alumni, a sound administrator with the trustees, a good speaker with the public, an astute bargainer with the foundations and the federal agencies, a politician with the state legislature, a friend of industry, labor, and agriculture, a persuasive diplomat with donors, a champion of education generally, a supporter of the professions (particularly law and medicine), a spokesman to the press, a scholar in his own right, a public servant at the state and national levels, a devotee of opera and football equally, a decent human being, a good husband and father, an active member of a church. Above all he must enjoy traveling in airplanes, eating his meals in public, and attending public ceremonies. No one can be all of these things. Some succeed at being none.

He should be firm, yet gentle; sensitive to others, insensitive to himself; look to the past and the future, yet be firmly planted in the present; both visionary and sound; affable, yet reflective; know the value of a dollar and realize that ideas cannot be bought; inspiring in his visions yet cautious in what he does; a man of principle yet able to make a deal; a man with broad perspective who will follow the details conscientiously; a good American but ready to criticize the status quo fearlessly; a seeker of truth where the truth may not hurt too much; a source of public policy pronouncements when they do not reflect on his own institution. He should sound like a mouse at home and look like a lion abroad. He is one of the marginal men in a democratic society— of whom there are many others—on the margin of many groups, many ideas, many endeavors, many characteristics. He is a marginal man but at the very center of the total process.

Who is he really?

To Flexner, he was a hero-figure, "a daring pioneer" who filled an "impossible post" yet some of his accomplishments were "little short of miraculous"; thus the "forceful president"—the Gilman, the Eliot, the Harper. The necessary revolutions came from on high. There should be Giants in the Groves. To Thorstein Veblen he was a "Captain of Erudition,"[14] and Veblen did not think well of captains. To Upton Sinclair, the university president was "the most universal faker and most variegated prevaricator that has yet appeared in the civilized world."[15]

To the faculty, he is usually not a hero-figure. Hutchins observed that the faculty really "prefer anarchy to any form of government"[16]—particularly the presidential form.

The issue is whether the president should be "leader" or "officeholder," as Hutchins phrased it; "educator" or "caretaker," as Harold W. Dodds[17] stated it; "creator" or "inheritor," as Frederick Rudolph[18] saw it; "initiator" as viewed by James L. Morrill[19] or consensus-seeker as viewed by John D. Millett;[20] the wielder of power or the persuader, as visualized by Henry M. Wriston;[21] "pump" or "bottleneck" as categorized by Eric Ashby.[22]

The case for leadership has been strongly put by Hutchins. A university needs a purpose, "a vision of the end." If it is to have a "vision," the president must identify it; and, without vision, there is "aimlessness" and the "vast chaos of the American university." "The administrator must accept a special responsibility for the discussion, clarification,

definition and proclamation of this end." He must
be a "troublemaker, for every change in education
is a change in the habits of some members of the
faculty." For all this he needs the great "moral
virtues" of "courage," "fortitude," "justice," and
"prudence." In looking for administrators who
really thought and wrote about the "end" of their
institution, Hutchins particularly identified Marcus
Aurelius as the great prototype.[23] Lowell, too,
believed a president should have a "plan" and that
although the faculty was "entitled to propose
changes," the plan should not basically be subject to
interference. He also had the rather quaint idea that
the president should "never feel hurried" or "work
. . . under pressure."[24]

There were such leaders in higher education.
Hutchins was one. Lowell was another; and so was
Eliot. When Eliot was asked by a faculty member of
the medical school how it could be after eighty years
of managing its own affairs the faculty had to
accommodate to so many changes, he could answer,
"There is a new president."[25] Even in Oxford, of all
places, as it belatedly adapted to the new world of
scholarship, Benjamin Jowett as Master of Balliol
could set as his rule: "Never retract, never explain.
Get it done and let them howl."[26] Lord Bryce could
comment in his *American Commonwealth* on the great
authority of the president in the American university, on his "almost monarchical position."[27]

But the day of the monarchs has passed—the day

when Benjamin Ide Wheeler could ride his white horse across the Berkeley campus or Nicholas Murray Butler rule from Morningside Heights. Flexner rather sadly recorded that "the day of the excessively autocratic president is . . . over. He has done a great service . . ." Paul Lazarsfeld could observe the "academic power vacuum" that resulted —leadership no longer taken by the president nor assumed by the faculty, with the result of little "institutional development."[28] Hutchins was the last of the giants in the sense that he was the last of the university presidents who really tried to change his institution and higher education in any fundamental way. Instead of the not always so agreeable autocracy, there is now the usually benevolent bureaucracy, as in so much of the rest of the world. Instead of the Captain of Erudition or even David Riesman's "staff sergeant," there is the Captain of the Bureaucracy who is sometimes a galley slave on his own ship; and "no great revolutionary figure is likely to appear."[29]

The role of giant was never a happy one. Hutchins concluded that the administrator has many ways to lose, and no way to win, and came to acknowledge that patience, which he once called a "delusion and a snare," was also a virtue. "It is one thing to get things done. It is another to make them last." The experience of Tappan at Michigan was typical of many, as Angell later saw it: "Tappan was the largest figure of a man that ever appeared on the Michigan campus. And he was stung to death by gnats."[30]

The giant was seldom popular with the faculty and was often bitterly opposed, as in the "revolution" against Wheeler at California. And faculty government gained strength as faculties gained distinction. The experiences of Tappan, Wheeler, Hutchins, even Thomas Jefferson, are part of the lore of the university presidency. So are those of Wayland, who resigned from Brown in frustration after vainly trying something new, Woodrow Wilson with all his battles over innovations at Princeton, and many others.

Moreover, the university has changed; it has become bigger and more complex, more tensed with checks and balances. As Rudolph saw it, there came to be "a delicate balance of interests, a polite tug of war, a blending of emphases." The presidency was "an office fraught with so many perils, shot through with so many ambiguities, an office that was many things to many men."[31] There are more elements to conciliate, fewer in a position to be led. The university has become the multiversity and the nature of the presidency has followed this change.

Also, the times have changed. The giants were innovators during a wave of innovation, to use the terms of Joseph Schumpeter drawn from another context. The American university required vast renovation to meet the needs of the changing and growing nation. As Eliot said in his inaugural address, "The University must accommodate itself promptly to significant changes in the character of the people for whom it exists." The title of Wilson's inaugural address was, "Princeton for the Nation's Service." They and others helped take what had been denominational colleges and turn them into modern national universities. They were not inventors—the Germans did the inventing—but they came along at a stage in history when massive innovation was the order of the day. The giants today, when found at all, are more likely to be in a few of the old Latin American universities undergoing modernization or the new British universities in the midst of an intense discussion of educational policy.

The giants had performed "a great service," but gentler hands were needed. University administration reverted to the more standard British model of "government by consent and after consultation."[32] There is a "kind of lawlessness"[33] in any large university with many separate sources of initiative and power; and the task is to keep this lawlessness within reasonable bounds. The president must seek "consensus" in a situation where there is a "struggle for power" among groups that share it.[34] "The president must use power economically, and persuasion to the fullest extent."[35] As Allan Nevins sees it, "The sharpest strain on growth lies not in finding the teachers, but expert administrators," and the new type of president required by the large universities "will be a coordinator rather than a creative leader . . . an expert executive, a tactful moderator. . . ."[36]

Academic government has taken the form of the Guild, as in the colleges of Oxford and Cambridge until recent times; of the Manor, as in Columbia under Butler; and of the United Nations, as in the modern multiversity. There are several "nations" of students, of faculty, of alumni, of trustees, of public groups. Each has its territory, its jurisdiction, its form of government. Each can declare war on the others; some have the power of veto. Each can settle its own problems by a majority vote, but altogether they form no single constituency. It is a pluralistic society with multiple cultures. Coexistence is more likely than unity. Peace is one priority item, progress another.

The president in the multiversity is leader, educator, creator, initiator, wielder of power, pump; he is *also* officeholder, caretaker, inheritor, consensus-seeker, persuader, bottleneck. But he is mostly a mediator.

The first task of the mediator is peace—how he may "the Two-and-Seventy jarring Sects confute." Peace within the student body, the faculty, the trustees; and peace between and among them. Peace between the "Two Cultures" and the "Three Cultures" and their subcultures; among all the ideas competing for support. Peace between the internal environment of the academic community and the external society that surrounds and sometimes almost engulfs it. But peace has its attributes. There is the "workable compromise" of the day that resolves the current problem. Beyond this lies the effective solution that enhances the long-run distinction and character of the institution. In seeking it, there are some things that should not be compromised, like freedom and quality—then the mediator needs to become the gladiator. The dividing lines between these two roles may not be as clear as crystal, but they are at least as fragile.

The second task is progress; institutional and personal survival are not enough. A multiversity is inherently a conservative institution but with radical functions. There are so many groups with a legitimate interest in the status quo, so many veto groups; yet the university must serve a knowledge explosion and a population explosion simultaneously. The president becomes the central mediator among the values of the past, the prospects for the future, and the realities of the present. He is the mediator among groups and institutions moving at different rates of speed and sometimes in different directions; a carrier of change—as infectious and sometimes as feared as a "Typhoid Mary." He is not an innovator for the sake of innovation, but he must be sensitive to the fruitful innovation. He has no new and bold "vision of the end." He is driven more by necessity than by voices in the air. "Innovation" may be the historical "measurement of success," the great characterizing feature of the "giants of the past";[37] but innovations sometimes succeed best when they have no obvious author. Lowell once observed that a president "cannot both do things and get credit for them"—that he should not "cackle like a hen that laid an egg."

The ends are already given—the preservation of the eternal truths, the creation of new knowledge, the improvement of service wherever truth and knowledge of high order may serve the needs of man. The ends are there; the means must be ever improved in a competitive dynamic environment. There is no single "end" to be discovered; there are several ends and many groups to be served.

The quality of the mediation is subject to judgment on two grounds, the keeping of the peace and the furthering of progress—the resolution of inter-personal and inter-group warfare, and the reconciliation of the tug of the anchor to the past with the pull of the Holy Grail of the future. Unfortunately peace and progress are more frequently enemies than friends; and since, in the long run, progress is more important than peace to a university, the effective mediator must, at times, sacrifice peace to progress. The ultimate test is whether the mediation permits progress to be made fast enough and in the right directions, whether the needed innovations take precedence over the conservatism of the institution. Mediators, though less dramatic than giants, are not a homogenized group; they only look that way.

They also appear to some people to be doing very little of consequence. Yet their role is absolutely essential if carried out constructively. They serve something of the function of the clerk of the meeting for the Quakers—the person who keeps the business moving, draws forth ideas, seeks the "sense of the meeting." David Riesman has suggested the term "evocator." The techniques must be those of the mediator; but to the techniques may also be added the goals of the innovator. The essence of the role, when adequately performed, is perhaps best conveyed by the term "mediator-initiator."

Power is not necessary to the task, though there must be a consciousness of power. The president must police its use by the constituent groups, so that none will have too much or too little or use it too unwisely. To make the multiversity work really effectively, the moderates need to be in control of each power center and there needs to be an attitude of tolerance between and among the power centers, with few territorial ambitions. When the extremists get in control of the students, the faculty, or the trustees with class warfare concepts, then the "delicate balance of interests" becomes an actual war.

The usual axiom is that power should be commensurate with responsibility, but, for the president, the *opportunity to persuade* should be commensurate with the responsibility. He must have ready access to each center of power, a fair chance in each forum of opinion, a chance to paint reality in place of illusion and to argue the cause of reason as he sees it.

Not all presidents seek to be constructive mediators amid their complexities. One famous president of a New York university succeeded in being at home only five months in five years. Some find it more pleasant to attend meetings, visit projects abroad, even give lectures at other universities; and at home they attend ceremonial functions, go to the local clubs, and allow the winds of controversy to swirl past them. Others look for "visions." But most presidents are in the control tower helping the real pilots make their landings without crashes, even in the fog.

Hutchins wrote of the four moral virtues for a university president. I should like to suggest a slightly different three—judgment, courage, and fortitude—but the greatest of these is fortitude since others have so little charity. The mediator, whether in government or industry or labor relations or domestic quarrels, is always subject to some abuse. He wins few clear-cut victories; he must aim more at avoiding the worst than seizing the best. He must find satisfaction in being *equally* distasteful to each of his constituencies; he must reconcile himself to the harsh reality that successes are shrouded in silence while failures are spotlighted in notoriety. The president of the multiversity must be content to hold its constituent elements loosely together and to move the whole enterprise another foot ahead in what often seems an unequal race with history.

LIFE IN THE MULTIVERSITY

The "Idea of a University" was a village with its priests. The "Idea of a Modern University" was a town—a one-industry town—with its intellectual oligarchy. "The Idea of a Multiversity" is a city of infinite variety. Some get lost in the city; some rise to the top within it; most fashion their lives within one of its many subcultures. There is less sense of community than in the village but also less sense of confinement. There is less sense of purpose than within the town but there are more ways to excel. There are also more refuges of anonymity— both for the creative person and the drifter. As against the village and the town, the "city" is more like the totality of civilization as it has evolved and more an integral part of it; and movement to and from the surrounding society has been greatly accelerated. As in a city, there are many separate endeavors under a single rule of law.

The students in the "city" are older, more likely to be married, more vocationally oriented, more drawn from all classes and races than the students in the village;[38] and they find themselves in a most intensely competitive atmosphere. They identify less with the total community and more with its subgroups. Burton R. Clark and Martin Trow have a particularly interesting typology of these subcultures: the "collegiate" of the fraternities and sororities and the athletes and activities majors; the "academic" of the serious students; the "vocational" of the students seeking training for specific jobs; and the "nonconformist" of the political activists, the aggressive intellectuals, and the bohemians.[39] These subcultures are not mutually exclusive, and some of the fascinating pageantry of the multiversity is found in their interaction one on another.

The multiversity is a confusing place for the student. He has problems of establishing his identity and sense of security within it. But it offers him a vast range of choices, enough literally to stagger the mind. In this range of choices he encounters the opportunities and the dilemmas of freedom. The casualty rate is high. The walking wounded are many. *Lernfreiheit*—the freedom of the student to pick and choose, to stay or to move on—is triumphant.

Life has changed also for the faculty member. The multiversity is in the main stream of events. To the teacher and the researcher have been added the consultant and the administrator. Teaching is less central than it once was for most faculty members; research has become more important. This has given rise to what has been called the "nonteacher" [40]—"the higher a man's standing, the less he has to do with students"—and to a threefold class structure of what used to be "the faculty": those who only do research, those who only teach (and they are largely in an auxiliary role), and those who still do some of both. In one university I know, the proportions at the Ph.D. level or its equivalent are roughly one researcher to two teachers to four who do both.

Consulting work and other sources of additional income have given rise to what is called the "affluent professor," a category that does include some but by no means all of the faculty. Additionally, many faculty members, with their research assistants and teaching assistants, their departments and institutes, have become administrators. A professor's life has become, it is said, "a rat race of business and activity, managing contracts and projects, guiding teams and assistants, bossing crews of technicians, making numerous trips, sitting on committees for government agencies, and engaging in other distractions necessary to keep the whole frenetic business from collapse." [41]

The intellectual world has been fractionalized as interests have become much more diverse; and there are fewer common topics of conversation at the faculty clubs. Faculty government has become more cumbersome, more the avocation of active minorities; and there are real questions whether it can work effectively on a large scale, whether it can agree on more than preservation of the status quo.

Faculty members are less members of the particular university and more colleagues within their national academic discipline groups.

But there are many compensations. "The American professoriate" is no longer, as Flexner once called it, "a proletariat." Salaries and status have risen considerably. The faculty member is more a fully participating member of society, rather than a creature on the periphery; some are at the very center of national and world events. Research opportunities have been enormously increased. The faculty member within the big mechanism and with all his opportunities has a new sense of independence from the domination of the administration or his colleagues; much administration has been effectively decentralized to the level of the individual professor. In particular, he has a choice of roles and mixtures of roles to suit his taste as never before. He need not leave the Groves for the Acropolis unless he wishes; but he can, if he wishes. He may even become, as some have, essentially a professional man with his home office and basic retainer on the campus of the multiversity but with his clients scattered from coast to coast. He can also even remain the professor of old, as many do. There are several patterns of life from which to choose. So the professor too has greater freedom. *Lehrfreiheit*, in the old German sense of the freedom of the professor to do as he pleases, also is triumphant.

What is the justification of the modern American

multiversity? History is one answer. Consistency with the surrounding society is another. Beyond that, it has few peers in the preservation and dissemination and examination of the eternal truths; no living peers in the search for new knowledge; and no peers in all history among institutions of higher learning in serving so many of the segments of an advancing civilization. Inconsistent internally as an institution, it is consistently productive. Torn by change, it has the stability of freedom. Though it has not a single soul to call its own, its members pay their devotions to truth.

The multiversity in America is perhaps best seen at work, adapting and growing, as it responded to the massive impact of federal programs beginning with World War II. A vast transformation has taken place without a revolution, for a time almost without notice being taken. The multiversity has demonstrated how adaptive it can be to new opportunities for creativity; how responsive to money; how eagerly it can play a new and useful role; how fast it can change while pretending that nothing has happened at all; how fast it can neglect some of its ancient virtues. What are the current realities of the federal grant university?

2

THE REALITIES OF THE FEDERAL GRANT UNIVERSITY

Two great impacts, beyond all other forces, have molded the modern American university system and made it distinctive. Both impacts have come from sources outside the universities. Both have come primarily from the federal government. Both have come in response to national needs.

The first was the land grant movement. Abraham Lincoln signed the Morrill Act in 1862. This act set the tone for the development of American universities, both public and private, for most of the ensuing hundred years. It was one of the most seminal pieces of legislation ever enacted.

The land grant movement came in response to the rapid industrial and agricultural development of the United States that attained such momentum in the middle of the last century. Universities were to assist this development through training that went beyond the creation of "gentlemen," and of teachers, preachers, lawyers, and doctors; through research related to the technical advance of farming and manufacturing; through service to many and ultimately to almost all of the economic and political segments of society. The land grant movement was also responsive to a growing democratic, even egalitarian and populist, trend in the nation. Pursuing this trend, higher education was to be open to all qualified young people from all walks of life. It was to serve less the perpetuation of an elite class and more the creation of a relatively classless society, with the doors of opportunity open to all through education.

This was a dramatic break with earlier American traditions in higher education. It created a new social force in world history. Nowhere before had universities been so closely linked with the daily life of so much of their societies. The university campus came to be one of the most heavily traveled crossroads in America—an intersection traversed by farmers, businessmen, politicians, students from almost every corner of almost every state. The cloister and the ivory tower were destroyed by being thrown open to all qualified comers.

Supporting the impact of the land grant movement was the effect on American universities of the model supplied by Germany. This German model gave academic respectability and content to the "land grant" idea; and Harvard, a private university with a long academic tradition, could travel much the same path of development as Cornell, a newly established land grant institution. German intellectualism and American populism were merged in the new university. Pure intellect and raw pragmatism made an unlikely but successful alliance.

The second great impact on the universities began with federal support of scientific research during World War II. The wartime laboratories that were the forerunners of such continuing government-financed research centers as the Lincoln Laboratory at the Massachusetts Institute of Technology, the Argonne at Chicago, and the Lawrence Radiation Laboratory at California, opened a new age. The major universities were enlisted in national defense and in scientific and technological development as never before. (In World War I the universities had only been a source of raw recruits.)

Instead of Gilman, Eliot, and White, there were now such new pioneers as Conant, Compton, and Bush to guide this alliance of the federal government with the universities. Don K. Price notes that "in the hands of Vannevar Bush, James B. Conant, and Karl T. Compton the government contract became a new type of federalism." [1] In addition to the industrial revolution there was now the scientific revolution to be served. In addition to the stimulus of Germany, there was Russia—for Russian scientific achievements both before and after Sputnik were an immense spur to the new departure. American universities have been changed almost as much by the federal research grant as by the land grant idea.

It is interesting that American universities, which pride themselves on their autonomy, should have taken their special character as much or more from the pressures of their environment as from their own inner desires; that institutions which identify themselves either as "private" or as "state" should have found their greatest stimulus in federal initiative; that universities which are part of a highly decentralized and varied system of higher education should, nevertheless, have responded with such fidelity and alacrity to national needs; that institutions which had their historical origins in the training of "gentlemen" should have committed themselves so fully to the service of brute technology.

The "federal grant" university has been emerging over the past twenty years, but until recently it has developed more by force of circumstances than by conscious design. The universities most affected have been making largely piecemeal adjustments to the new phenomena without any great effort at an overall view of what has been happening to them. Perhaps this was just as well—the transition probably was smoother precisely because it was not subjected to critical analysis. The federal government and the leading universities entered into a common-law marriage unblessed by predetermined policies and self-surveys—but nonetheless they formed a very productive union.

All this, however, as was inevitable, is being changed. Harvard has now studied itself. So has Princeton. Brookings and Carnegie have studied us all; so have the Department of Health, Education, and Welfare; the President's Science Advisory Committee; the American Council on Education; and the American Assembly.[2] The principal conclusion was predictable: the federal colossus had the power to influence the most ruggedly individual of universities. A paradox emerged: the better and the more individual the university, the greater its chances of succumbing to the federal embrace. Washington did not waste its money on the second-rate.

Soon there will be a national policy as well as nationwide activity, and I am at least a little concerned. All these studies have identified problems that we knew all along to exist. But now that we have publicly identified the problems, we shall be expected to deal with them; and in dealing with them we shall create new problems. Mostly, we shall have to strive for "balance" in a number of different ways. We shall have to "balance" the wishes of individual scholars with those of their institutions; New England with the South; the sciences with the humanities; research with teaching;

graduate training with undergraduate education; merit with politics; the judgment of specialists with general formulae. And yet one of the more productive aspects of federal involvement to date has been its imbalance.

We are clearly entering the second phase of the "federal grant" development. The first I shall identify as the phase of "intuitive imbalance," and the new phase just emerging as one of "bureaucratic balance." It is a good time to examine where we have been and where we may be going. We are in the midst of a vast transformation of university life and none of us can be too sure where we really are going; but we can try to peer ahead.

As a basis for discussing the two phases of federal grant development, I shall briefly review the essential facts about federal involvement with universities in this country.

¶ Federal interest in higher education dates from 1787. That year saw the beginning of endowment of public institutions of higher education with public lands, following the example of the Northwest Ordinance of 1785, which provided land to support public schools at the lower levels. However, this interest was not made effective until the Morrill Land Grant Act of 1862. Then the Second Morrill Act in 1890 supplemented the original land grants with federal grants of funds to support college instruction in specified subjects; these grants still continue, and, in fact, have recently been expanded.

Federal interest in higher education was further
made effective by the Hatch Act in 1887, establishing the Agricultural Experiment Stations, and by
the Smith-Lever Act in 1914, creating the Agricultural Extension Service. During World War I, the
ROTC program was established. During the Great
Depression, universities were involved in the programs of the Work Projects Administration and
National Youth Administration. During World
War II, universities participated heavily in the
Engineering, Science and Management War Training Program inaugurated in 1940. In that same
year, the National Defense Research Committee
(later the Office of Scientific Research and Development) was established, and leading universities became engaged in the various programs of war research which it set up.

After World War II and again after the Korean
conflict, the "G.I. Bill" and the corresponding bill
for Korean veterans sent a seismic shock through
academic life.

Despite this long history of federal interest, however, it is evident that with the exception of the
comparatively restricted areas of agriculture and
military training, there was no continuing federal
involvement with higher education until World
War II.

¶ Currently, federal support has become a major
factor in the total performance of many universities,
and the sums involved are substantial. Higher edu-

cation in 1960 received about $1.5 billion from the
federal government—a hundredfold increase in
twenty years. About one third of this $1.5 billion
was for university-affiliated research centers; about
one third for project research within universities;
and about one third for other things, such as residence hall loans, scholarships, and teaching programs. This last third was expended at colleges as
well as universities, but the first two thirds almost
exclusively at universities, and at relatively few of
them.

The $1 billion for research, though only 10 per-
cent of total federal support for research and development, accounted for 75 percent of all university
expenditures on research and 15 percent of total
university budgets. Clearly the shape and nature
of university research are profoundly affected by
federal monies.

¶ Federal research funds to universities flow
primarily from six agencies. In 1961 the percentage
distribution was as follows:

Department of Health, Education, and Welfare . . 39
(37 percent was from National Institutes of Health alone)
Department of Defense 32
National Science Foundation 11
Atomic Energy Commission 8
Department of Agriculture 6
National Aeronautics and Space
    Administration 3
Other agencies 1

(These figures do not include funds for university-operated government research centers.)

This federal support has been almost exclusively identified with three great and somewhat inter-related national concerns: defense (40 percent of the total in 1961, including support by the Department of Defense and the Atomic Energy Commission); scientific and technological progress (20 percent—National Science Foundation, Department of Agriculture, and NASA); and health (37 percent—through the National Institutes of Health). Federal support has not been directed explicitly toward strengthening universities generally, or one or more universities specifically, in any over-all fashion—as might be said of the University Grants Committee in Great Britain.

¶ Federal research expenditures have been largely restricted to the physical and biomedical sciences, and engineering, with only about 3 percent for the social sciences and hardly any support for the humanities.

¶ Among the totality of university functions, federal support has been heavily concentrated on research and on graduate and postdoctoral training in fields of national interest.

¶ The preferred approach of the federal government to the use of university facilities for research has been (a) the specialized research center—by 1963 there were fourteen major ones,[3] and (b) the research project. Projects have been supported for relatively short terms and specific purposes; and support has been awarded, usually on the advice of qualified experts, on the basis of prospective performance.

¶ Federal research expenditures have been heavily focused on a relatively few institutions. If both project research and large research centers are included, six universities received 57 percent of the funds in a recent fiscal year, and twenty universities received 79 percent. If project research alone is considered, the figures are 28 and 54 percent. As a percentage of total university expenditures for all purposes among the leading twenty recipients, federal funds have amounted to 20 to 50 percent when project research alone is counted and from 20 to over 80 percent when the research centers are added. These twenty universities are only about one tenth of all universities in the United States. They constitute the primary federal grant universities.

¶ Recently there has been some spreading out of federal interest from the physical and biomedical to the social sciences; from graduate to undergraduate training; from a selective few to an expanded number of universities.

PHASE ONE: INTUITIVE IMBALANCE

For about twenty years now, Congress has been deciding in which general areas the partnership between the federal government and the universities should be developed. The areas chosen have been defense, scientific and technological progress, and health. Decisions have not been based on thorough study of national priorities. They have been made pragmatically, in response to the felt needs of the nation and of the people in accord with the possibilities of the times, and also, to an extent, in response to the urgings of very powerful lobbies. The atom was split, and could be used for war and peace. The "cold war" followed World War II and necessitated further defense work. Health became a matter of great national concern. Possibilities for space exploration developed. Congress reacted quickly to each of these realities.

Once Congress initiated a program, federal administrative officers turned to those universities best able to give immediate and effective assistance on the individual programs; or rather they turned to those scientists in the best position to respond quickly and efficiently—and those scientists were principally located in a limited number of institutions. These actions were not undertaken on the basis of any general review of institutional capacity or potential capacity, but on quick and ready apprehension of possibilities and response to them. The test was who could most effectively do the job at hand. The process was more intuitive than studied.

For about twenty years, universities have been accepting the research centers and projects as proposed by faculty members and government agencies, making such day-to-day adjustments as were needed and possible. In consequence, these universities have been profoundly affected. The whole process has been one of starting new endeavors, and this has changed the pre-existing "balance" in several ways. Some real and some not so real issues have arisen for the universities.

1. *Federal control and federal influence.* Federal control as a substantive issue is, as Sidney Hook has said, a "red herring."[4] With a few exceptions—the generally necessary exception of secrecy in certain types of work and the unnecessary exception of the disclaimer affidavit required by the National Defense Education Act—there has been no control in any deleterious sense. By way of contrast, state control of state universities has been a real problem.[5] The federal government has customarily put scientifically trained persons in charge of science programs and they have operated fully within academic traditions.

The real problem is not one of federal control but of federal influence. A federal agency offers a project. A university need not accept—but, as a practical matter, it usually does. One of the quickest ways to lose a faculty member is by refusing to accept the grant he has just negotiated with his counterpart in Washington. Out of this reality have followed many of the consequences of federal aid for the universities; and they have been substantial. That they are subtle, slowly cumulative and gentlemanly makes them all the more potent.

2. *University control and the agency as alma mater.* A university's control over its own destiny has been substantially reduced. University funds from tuition and fees, gifts and endowments, and state sources go through the usual budget-making procedures and their assignment is subject to review in accordance with internal policy. Federal research funds, however, are usually negotiated by the individual scholar with the particular agency, and so bypass the usual review process. Thus 20 to 50 to 80 percent of a university's expenditures may be handled outside the normal channels. These funds in turn commit some of the university's own funds; they influence the assignment of space; they determine the distribution of time between teaching and research; to a large extent they establish the areas in which the university grows the fastest. Almost imperceptibly, a university is changed.

The authority of the department chairman, the dean, the president is thereby reduced; so also is the role of faculty government. This may have its advantages. Scholars seem to prefer dealing with their professional counterparts in Washington rather than with their colleagues and administrators at home.[6] Also the university's internal process of distributing funds would be generally less selective and less flexible than the federal research project approach. Within a university, the tendency is to give each faculty member about the same opportunity and once having given it to keep giving it thereafter; but the project method allows more attention to exceptional merit and has the advantage that all projects may end some time. Additionally, federal agencies are more responsive to particular national needs than the universities would be, given the same amount of money to spend according to their own priority system.

There are, however, clearly detrimental effects. Some faculty members come to use the pressure of their agency contacts against their university. They may try to force the establishment of a new administrative unit or the assignment of land for their own special building, in defiance of general university policy or priorities. These pressures, of course, should be withstood; they speak well neither of the professor nor of the agency. Also, some faculty members tend to shift their identification and loyalty from their university to the agency in Washington. Their concern with the general welfare of the university is eroded and they become tenants rather than owners, taking their grants with them as they change their institutional lodgings. The university, as Allen Wallis, president of the University of Rochester, has remarked, becomes to an extent a "hotel." The agency becomes the new alma mater. The research entrepreneur becomes a euphoric schizophrenic.

It has been said that, in the face of federal aid,

university presidents have "abdicated" their responsibilities for the general conduct of their institutions. I would put it differently—they have let some things go by that they would have liked to do differently; but this is often what they do anyway. There are, however, especially acute problems when the agency insists on the tie-in sale (if we do this for you, then you must do that for us) or when it requires frequent and detailed progress reports. Then the university really is less than a free agent. It all becomes a kind of "putting-out" system with the agency taking the place of the merchant-capitalist of old. Sweat shops have developed out of such a system in earlier times and in other industries.

3. *"Scientists Affluent, Humanists Militant."*[7] Federal research support has added a new dimension to the eternal class struggles within a university. To student versus faculty, assistant versus tenure professors, and faculty versus administrators has been added a new hierarchical point of tension—that between humanists and scientists. The scientists, by and large, in the federal grant universities, get promoted faster, get more space, get more income through summer employment and consulting, have more secretaries and assistants, have greater access to travel funds and expense accounts, and accumulate a greater sense of status within and outside the academic community. Some humanists obviously resent all this and consider it quite unfair, even

though their own situation has improved, relative to
what it used to be.

However, there is still another side to the story.
The scientist who gets a series of projects going can
become caught in his own apparatus. Graduate
students and staff members become dependent upon
him. He is committed to project deadlines and
periodic contract negotiations. He is enmeshed in a
web of obligations and it is very hard to break out.
As a result, he often works hard at things he would
rather not do—more often than need be true of the
humanist.

There is some current tendency for the brightest
of graduate students to prefer the sciences to the
social sciences and the humanities,[8] and this will
have an impact on comparative faculty quality as
between fields of study in the years to come. How
much of this has been caused by federal aid and how
much by the current liveliness of the different fields
is not at all clear. My own impression is that the
brightest graduate students flock to the areas with
the brightest new ideas, regardless of federal aid.

All this is said to have destroyed the "balance"
among fields and it is generally concluded that
something should be done about it. The balance
among fields, however, has never been a static thing.
If it were, philosophy, theology, and the classics
would still be the dominant areas of study, as they
have not been for a long time. Assuming that the

balance of 1942, say, was appropriate for 1942, this does not mean it would have been appropriate for 1962. It is not enough to say that the old "balance" has been destroyed. The real question is what should be the proper balance today? It is clear that the flowering of the Renaissance should have affected the "balance" in the sixteenth century. It would seem likely that the splitting of the atom and the deciphering of the genetic code should in their turn affect the balance of the twentieth century. We should expect the most money and the brightest students and the greatest prestige to follow the most exciting new ideas. By and large they have done so, and this is one way of defining the nature of balance. (Economics was exciting in the 1930's; sociology was more exciting in the 1950's.)

The real question, it seems to me, is not one of balance in any historical or monetary sense, but rather what is most appropriate to each field in each period. "All fields are equal, only some are more equal than others." There should be no effort to do the same things in the same amounts for each field. Each should receive support in accordance with its current potentialities, and potentialities vary. There are no timeless priorities.

The academic community has lived with inequities before. Agriculture in the land grant institutions has had eleven-month appointments, low teaching loads, and heavy research subsidies for decades. Law and medicine have reflected within the academic world some of the power and affluence of their professions in the outside world. These are stated as matters of fact, not as ideal situations.

Generally, I think, it is remarkable and commendable that so high a degree of internal equity has thus far been preserved within the academic world in the face of quite chaotic pressures impinging upon it.

4. *The inevitability of concentration.* The project approach almost automatically led to concentration of federal research effort in a relatively few universities. The universities best equipped to undertake the research were also those with the faculty and facilities to provide for the training of Ph.D.'s. It is no coincidence that the six universities with a little more than 25 percent of project funds graduated about 25 percent of the Ph.D.'s; and a similar situation prevails for the top twenty universities. If "only the best will do,"[9] this concentration of effort is inevitable. A different result would have been quite surprising.

This concentration of effort has undoubtedly strengthened the facilities and improved the quality of faculties of universities already in the front rank. It has probably widened the gap between those of the first and those of the second and third ranks. It may, in fact, have actually injured universities of the second and third ranks and some colleges by turning their potential faculty members into research personnel in the front-rank universities. The good are better; the poor may well be worse. And it has greatly accentuated the differences between colleges and universities.

5. *Teaching the graduates versus teaching the undergraduates.* The much-advertised conflict between teaching and research puts the problem the wrong way. The teaching of graduate students is so closely tied to research that if research is improved, graduate instruction is almost bound to be improved also. And the almost universal experience seems to be that federal research support has improved graduate instruction. There have been better facilities, more research assistantships and fellowships, more research projects in which students can work directly with faculty members—all resulting from federal funds. At the graduate level, there has been a clear gain, and fortunately so, because graduate enrollments at the federal grant universities have been increasing rapidly.

At the undergraduate level, however, the "subtle discounting of the teaching process"[10] has been aided and abetted. Harold Orlans, who conducted the excellent Brookings study of federal aid to universities, concludes that federal research aid "has accelerated the long-standing depreciation of undergraduate education at large universities."[11] This is my own observation, with one exception—that a very few private institutions with long traditions of very high-quality undergraduate instruction have been able to maintain their standards; and this is to their great credit.

The reasons for the general deterioration of undergraduate teaching are several. Teaching loads and student contact hours have been reduced. Faculty members are more frequently on leave or temporarily away from the campus; some are never more than temporarily on campus. More of the instruction falls to teachers who are not members of the regular faculty. The best graduate students prefer fellowships and research assistantships to teaching assistantships. Postdoctoral fellows who might fill the gap usually do not teach. Average class size has been increasing.

There seems to be a "point of no return" after which research, consulting, graduate instruction become so absorbing that faculty efforts can no longer be concentrated on undergraduate instruction as they once were. This process has been going on for a long time; federal research funds have intensified it. As a consequence, undergraduate education in the large university is more likely to be acceptable than outstanding; educational policy from the undergraduate point of view is largely neglected. How to escape the cruel paradox that a superior faculty results in an inferior concern for undergraduate teaching is one of our more pressing problems.

6. *The faculty and the un-faculty.* University scholars

traditionally have both taught and conducted research. But now some scholars are added to the staff in exclusively research capacities—and increasingly with titles suggesting professorial status. They have no teaching responsibilities and are not as yet fully accepted members of the academic community. They usually are not members of the Academic Senate and they usually are not given tenure—both traditional marks of faculty status. In many institutions, however, they may use the name of the university in getting projects under their own direction.

In a far less anomalous position is the faculty member who works on a federally sponsored project during the summer months and part-time during the regular year, and receives much of his pay from the project rather than from the university. But to what extent is he really a university employee and what security of employment does he really have? Obviously, it is no longer so clear as it once was just who is the faculty.

There has been an almost frantic remaking of the rules—new titles created, new relationships established, new classes of citizenship formulated and only partially assimilated. The Harvard catalogue now lists more than 5,000 "Officers of Instruction and Administration," many of whom are not faculty in the traditional sense. The "faculty" in our universities becomes an ever-changing group as the definitions change. If there can still be said to be a "faculty" at all, it is most certainly a different composite than before. Much of the teaching, much of the research is done by the "un-faculty."

7. *University "aid" to the federal government.* Federal aid has been of great benefit to the universities. It has not, however, been without its costs in money and effort. Overhead allowances vary greatly from agency to agency but seldom cover all the indirect as well as the direct costs of sponsored research. Also, matching grants for construction may force a university to upset its own priority system in order to get federal funds. This, of course, is the intent.

Additionally, federal funds have placed great new administrative burdens on the universities—on faculty members, on department chairmen, on deans, on presidents. New classes of administrators have been created—the contracting officer and the research project manager. Administration becomes a much larger aspect of the total university enterprise. Julius A. Stratton has observed, "There is a basic incompatibility between the true spirit of a university and those elements of management which tend to creep into the organization of projects, the planning of programs, and the utilization of costly facilities."[12]

8. *On the borders of temptation.* Immense sums of money have been poured into the universities by the federal government, and universities are highly atomistic entities. The university has the responsibility for but usually not the actual control of these

funds. Some abuses have inevitably developed. Funds have been diverted at times from one use to another—and the other a use not intended by the federal agency. Some faculty members make informal alliances—if you consult on my project, then I should consult on yours—and total income has been pyramided through this exchange of consultancies to occasionally astounding levels. When these same faculty members sit on the federal panels that make the grants, the whole process becomes quite involved, to say the least. Excessive amounts of expensive equipment have at times been purchased, and equipment salesmen chase grants around. Some universities promise not only a base salary but substantial supplemental personal income and allowances from federal grants as a recruiting device in a wilder and wilder upward spiral.

There have been some scandals. There will be more. The federal agencies will exercise increasingly specific controls and the universities dependent on this new standard of living will accept these controls. The universities themselves will have to exercise more stringent controls by centralizing authority, particularly through the audit process. In a few situations, self-restraint has not been enough restraint; as one result, greater external restraint will be imposed in most situations.

With all its problems, however, federal research aid to universities has helped greatly in meeting national needs. It has greatly assisted the universities themselves. The nation is stronger. The leading universities are stronger. As Nathan Pusey reported the unanimous views of the presidents of universities participating in the Carnegie study, federal aid, over all, has been a "good thing."[13] In their turn, the federal grant universities have adapted to their new role quite quickly and effectively.

Professor Don Price has made reference to the following limerick:

> There was a young lady from Kent
> Who said that she knew what it meant
> When men took her to dine,
> Gave her cocktails and wine;
> She knew what it meant—but she went.[14]

I am not so sure that the universities and their presidents always knew what it meant; but one thing is certain—they went.

PHASE TWO: BUREAUCRATIC BALANCE

The general policy of federal agencies in allocating research grants to universities for the last two decades has been one of "seeking excellence wherever it is," one of accepting the established pattern and following it. The new approach is to take more of an over-all view; to change the pattern to a degree. Balance is the new virtue; imbalance the old sin.

The charge, made by Logan Wilson among others, has been that "There is no federal program

—merely programs."[15] The response—in the proposed "National Education Improvement Act of 1963," for example—is to provide: "A comprehensive program of Federal aid to meet selected and urgent needs of American education on all levels from elementary school through graduate education; to promote educational quality, expand opportunity for education, and to increase the capacity of our educational institutions; to provide for the Nation's needs in skilled manpower, national growth, and national security."

The new balance calls for developing a larger number of outstanding centers of graduate instruction and research. The Seaborg report suggested an expansion from the present fifteen or twenty centers to thirty or forty over a fifteen-year period.[16] The National Education Improvement Act envisages expansion from twenty to seventy. This demand for geographical dispersion of centers of strength follows, in part, the new realization of the role of a university as a factor influencing the location of industry. The Roswell L. Gilpatric report for the Department of Defense explained the concentration of defense contracts in California and Massachusetts by the concentration of research and development projects in these two states, which in turn was attributed to the availability of university centers of substantial strength.[17] An educational and political effort of considerable dimensions now seeks to reorder the current pattern of distribution in the name of balance.

Under the National Defense Education Act of 1958, preference is already given to assisting *new* graduate programs in selected subject matter areas. Teaching is being emphasized along with research. Summer refresher courses for teachers of science, improvement of science textbooks, and language laboratories are programs already well established. The National Science Foundation has a large effort under way to improve and renovate equipment for undergraduate teaching in the physical sciences. Undergraduates, as well as graduate students, are being assisted by loans and scholarships. The social sciences are receiving increasing sums of money. More funds are being granted to colleges as well as to universities, and to universities of all ranks. In particular, "institutional grants," to supplement project grants, are being given by the National Science Foundation and the National Institutes of Health. And NASA, among others, makes "training" grants to institutions instead of awarding fellowships to students who may then go wherever they wish. Thus, efforts to achieve greater "balance" are already well under way.

The approach to a university "as an institution" is of particular interest. If additional universities are to be selected to become centers of strength in research and graduate instruction, then it will be necessary for the federal government to be concerned with the "general health of the institution." This will be a notable departure from historical practice, except in agriculture. The Land Grant Association, in commenting on recent recommendations by the President's Science Advisory Committee for dispersion through assistance to institutions as such, said: "The recommendations represent a return to the principles of government-institution relations laid down in the basic land grant legislation, in which the responsibility for internal administration, fiscal management, and proper direction is vested with university officers rather than with agency staffs."[18] It should be noted that *every* state has at least one land grant institution receiving federal support on a formula basis. The parallel with agriculture is not entirely apt, however, since agriculture by its very nature is locally and regionally oriented, but national defense and space exploration are not.

If we are to move toward federal orientation to the "total function of the university," then the University Grants Committee in Great Britain is the outstanding precedent, and one that has received some support in the United States.[19] However, there are only about thirty universities in Great Britain and it is clear what is and what is not a university. Additionally, the University Grants Committee has come to exercise more influence over the establishment of new programs, the cost and size and even the appearance of new buildings, the equalization of faculty salaries among institutions, and the determination of admission policies than would currently be acceptable if it came from the federal government in this country.

Some hard choices must be faced. The decentralized project approach of the last two decades has much to recommend it. It is selective on merit, flexible in accordance with quality of performance, and responsive to national goals. The universities and their scholars retain substantial freedom. But such dominant reliance on the project approach is no longer likely. In fact, the project is already less the chosen instrument than it once was. Productive anarchy is no longer such a politically viable solution.

It is said that support to institutions as such will "give a university the necessary autonomy," and will permit dispersion of effort and better balance in several directions. It is not clear, however, how the particular institutions will be chosen, or, once chosen, how support might subsequently be withdrawn if performance should prove inadequate. It is difficult to assess the merit of a total institution as complex as a modern university. One alternative is to rely on a formula, as in the case of agriculture in the land grant institutions. Another is to be guided by political influence; and this is increasingly happening.

It is reported that Congress already senses its loss

of control to the professional personnel in the various agencies and would like to regain it. "Congress knows it has forfeited much power over science to the Executive and it does not like it."[20] The Harvard self-study report notes the danger of political interference and "log-rolling" inherent in block grants.[21] Inter-university competition would be taken from the quasi-academic arena of the agency committee to the legislative halls.

Additionally, the selection of designated "centers of strength" assumes a single source of designation —a single over-all federal agency or committee. A single agency means a single source of control, as against the current pluralistic situation of several agencies and several sources of influence, with opportunity to pick and choose among them. A single source of control would turn an influential relationship into a really "perilous partnership."[22] Finally, will funds necessarily be better spent for the national interest under institutional control than through the agencies, where decisions are freer from internal rigidities and egalitarian tendencies?

In the battle over institutional versus project support, Congressmen are more likely to prefer the institutional approach than are the professionals in the agencies; the presidents of universities than the researchers within the universities; the less well-established universities than the well-established ones; the humanists than the scientists—generally, those who have less under the project system than those who have more.

It is almost obligatory in educational circles these days to support "excellence" *and* "balance." They are the two magic words. Yet "excellence" and "balance" sometimes pull in different directions. It is also quite necessary to favor "institutional integrity" and to be against "federal control." Yet the institutional grants that aid what we are supposed to favor (integrity) may also aid what we are supposed to be against (control). Turning "integrity" over to the university president may also turn "control" over to the federal government.

How can we really best secure "aristocracy of achievement arising out of democracy of opportunity?"[23]

SOME SUGGESTIONS

The nation does face some grave problems in the field of education. Vastly increased numbers of students are pouring into our schools. Many qualitative deficiencies exist. State and local subdivisions are caught with relatively fixed tax structures, and private endowments and gifts have their limits also. Federal support is the most obvious way out. But federal expenditures themselves are not unlimited, and there are some realistic barriers to certain types of federal involvement.

The first consideration is that the federal government need not and cannot do everything. It seems to me that the educational system of America, good as it generally is, is in the most trouble—and thus in the greatest need of federal help—at the bottom and at the top.

At the bottom is the problem of "drop-outs" from school and "drop-outs" of the unskilled from the employed labor force. Through occupational training and retraining, through counseling, guidance, and relocation, these "drop-outs" should be assisted to acquire skills valuable in a dynamic economy where skill levels are rising at perhaps the fastest rate in history. Full employment is the necessary complement to make such training effective.

At the top, the nation needs more research activity in a number of fields and more personnel of high skill—particularly engineers, scientists, mathematicians, teachers, and medical doctors. A recent Bureau of Labor Statistics survey shows that from now to 1970 the expected supply of engineers and scientists will fill only three quarters of the demand. This leaves a very large gap. The prospect is particularly critical for engineers.

Fortunately the levels where federal aid is most necessary are levels where it is most politically feasible. My suggestions will be limited to higher education, and to the university level in particular.

1. Federal research centers, whenever possible, should be located near and identified with a univer-

sity. A university, with its libraries, colleagues to talk to, and graduate students to train, provides a uniquely favorable environment for such centers. In turn, such centers provide additional research opportunities for the university's faculty members and graduate students. Instead of establishing a research center in isolation and then, perhaps, having to build a new university at the same site, it seems to me best to put the center near some university— even if it doesn't happen to be our own.

2. The project system should be continued in essentially its present form as the major means of supporting the research and graduate instruction programs of universities as well as accomplishing the specific research purposes of the federal government. If project funds double or triple during the decade of the sixties, as now seems likely, it will be possible and necessary to extend more of them beyond the twenty institutions that constitute the primary group of federal grant universities at the present time. Orlans has identified about ten universities, mostly "public" ones, which already deserve considerably more project support on the basis of their existing Ph.D. programs.[24] Other universities will soon be moving into this group in the natural course of events. The project system follows established lines of contact through disciplines and avoids the problems of establishing a new reliance on institutional lines of contact.

The project system has resulted in a "highly

successful working relationship between the government's need for long- and short-term research and the academic scientist's abilities and interests."[25]

To the extent that institutional grants are given, they should follow the project grants. Charles V. Kidd has suggested that 25 percent might be given as free funds to institutions, as against 75 percent in project funds.[26] Twenty-five percent appears to be an adequate figure. These institutional grants could best be used by the universities for new projects, small projects, support of young faculty members unknown in Washington, and of fields neglected in direct federal grants—all on a very flexible basis. Thus the universities' rather different evaluation of "merit" could supplement the standards for merit of the federal agencies. I would hope that the institutional grants would be assigned automatically by the agencies as some percentage of the project grants which are themselves assigned on merit. If "quality must come first,"[27] this is the best way to assure it.

Alvin M. Weinberg has recently made the interesting suggestion that the panel system of reviewing research proposals could be improved as an instrument for making scientific judgments by including on the panels representatives of related fields, as well as representatives of the field in question. "I should think that advice from panels so constituted," he says, "would be tempered by concern for larger issues; in particular the support of a proposed research project would be viewed from the larger perspective of the relevance of that research to the rest of science."[28] The greater impartiality of the panels would also be assured.

Contract and grant overhead should cover reasonable indirect as well as all direct costs.

Federal project funds are increasingly being used to bid salaries and allowances up and to bid teaching assignments down. How much further such competition can go without raising grave policy problems for the federal agencies is problematical. The market is sufficiently active without this added inflationary stimulus; and the universities are sufficiently in trouble with internal inequities and reduction of teaching time.

There is currently arising a three-sided competitive struggle for research and development work, involving industry, the universities, and the government itself.[29] The universities should be preferred for basic research and for such other research as is readily related to graduate instruction.

It is being suggested, and also being implemented, that federal grants and contracts be channeled increasingly into liberal arts colleges to assist faculty research and the training of outstanding undergraduate students. This process can easily subvert the colleges from their primary obligation and start them on the way to becoming quite different types of institutions. With a project-by-project approach this is almost bound to happen. Would it not be well for the governing bodies of such colleges to examine the implications of this changed role before the process of project-by-project transformation of the nature of the institution is begun? If they accept the role they should accept it by a conscious policy decision.

3. To aid the teaching function of universities during the "deficit years" of greatly swollen enrollments just ahead, federal agencies should permit, even encourage, postdoctoral fellows and research professors to teach one-quarter or even one-third time at no cost to the institution. The present system increases the size of the "un-faculty" and widens the gap between the researcher and the student. Also, the further creation of research career professorships might well be examined. Are they really necessary from a research point of view and is it really desirable to preclude their occupants from normal participation in the full range of academic life?

The universities themselves should see to it that teaching assistantships are fully competitive with research assistantships and fellowships.

4. Federal agencies should provide space and equipment for their postdoctoral fellows and research career professors and for all contracts and most grants without the requirement of matching funds. It is very difficult to obtain space and equipment for these purposes from either endowments or state support, and also not entirely appropriate.

5. A National Foundation for Higher Education

might well be created on the model of the National Science Foundation. It could serve as a focal point for the interests of higher education and make grants outside the province of the National Science Foundation. Such a foundation would need to explore carefully the areas where support would be most productive, and also the appropriate forms of support, as did the National Science Foundation with such skill and judgment in its fields of interest. Areas for possible early consideration, as examples, are the creative arts, international studies, and environmental planning. Each is at a stage of considerable activity; each carries a high degree of national interest. Additionally, a Foundation for Higher Education might well undertake the support of great regional library resources with union catalogues made available to other university and college libraries in the region.

6. A number of other federal programs now in effect to aid higher education have generally worked well and should be continued.

The established program of the Federal Housing Authority in making loans for residence halls, student unions, and parking structures should be continued and expanded, as should the several programs under the National Defense Education Act. These programs are all widely dispersed in their efforts, and affect nearly all universities and many colleges.

Graduate fellowship programs should be expanded as there are capable graduate students to fill them. The availability of money does not by itself create a supply of competent candidates. At least half of the graduate fellowships should be transferable on a national basis, and not more than half tied to particular institutions. The practice of the Rockefeller Foundation and Woodrow Wilson Foundation of making an institutional grant to cover part of the institutional expenses for each scholar might well be more widely emulated.

The great need for curriculum reform in many fields, caused by the changing content and structure of knowledge growing out of research, should be recognized by federal agencies. They should support the efforts of universities to re-examine and improve the teaching in these areas. Some support is being given, particularly by the National Science Foundation in the physical sciences, but unfortunately some recent developments run counter to this trend. For example, the National Institutes of Health now cannot support any such efforts in the biological sciences—an area where they are greatly needed.

Foreign service projects conducted by universities for the federal government appear to be most fruitful if there is a major institutional assignment for a substantial period of time. *Ad hoc* projects accomplish little for the foreign country or for the contracting university.

7. Medical and dental doctors are in short supply

and will be in shorter supply. Fellowships and facilities for their training deserve high federal priority.[30]

8. A Council of Advisers on Education, as suggested by the American Assembly in 1960,[31] would provide an opportunity for an over-all view of the educational system and the educational needs of the nation as no single agency can do. This would be something like the President's Council of Economic Advisers, but in the educational field. Education may well need a better-coordinated voice than it has had, as McGeorge Bundy has so eloquently argued,[32] but the federal government also may need a more coordinated ear.

This council might assist in the preparation of a manpower budget covering the supply of, and demand for, the skills that depend on formal education. Indeed, beyond this the nation might benefit from an over-all manpower budget, supplementing its other budgets, for it would focus attention on human resources and on the importance of developing them.

The partnership of the federal government with higher education and particularly with the federal grant universities over the last two decades has been enormously productive in enlarging the pool of scientific ideas and skills. Now we are entering a new phase of widening and deepening relationships. This new phase can carry the American commitment to education to new heights of endeavor. It can also preserve the traditional freedom of higher education from excessive control. It can enlarge the horizons of equality of opportunity. It can maintain and even increase the margin for excellence. The challenge is to make certain it does all these things.

3

THE FUTURE OF THE
CITY OF INTELLECT

"THE true American University," David Starr Jordan once observed, "lies in the future." It still does; for American universities have not yet developed their full identity, their unique theory of purpose and function. They still look to older and to foreign models, although less and less; and the day is coming when these models will no longer serve at all.

The task of prophecy is made difficult by the many internal and external cross-currents to which universities are exposed. Archibald MacLeish wrote in 1941: "Like other private institutions, Harvard must face the fact that gifts to the university in the foreseeable future will not equal in bulk the gifts of the late twenties. Like other private institutions, it must admit that the peak of enrollment has probably been reached. And like other private institutions it must therefore accept the fact that this period of its history will be a period of organization within existing frontiers, rather than a period of extension of existing frontiers." [1] Since 1941 Harvard has become a federal grant university, has obtained private gifts beyond previous experience, has expanded far beyond its then "existing frontiers." This illustration serves to demonstrate that prophecy has its perils when treating with as dynamic an institution in as changing an environment as the modern American university.

THE SECOND TRANSFORMATION

The American university is currently undergoing its second great transformation. The first occurred during roughly the last quarter of the nineteenth century, when the land grant movement and German intellectualism were together bringing extraordinary change. The current transformation will cover roughly the quarter century after World War II. The university is being called upon to educate previously unimagined numbers of students; to respond to the expanding claims of national service; to merge its activities with industry as never before; to adapt to and rechannel new intellectual currents. By the end of this period, there will be a truly American university, an institution unique in world history, an institution not looking to other models but serving, itself, as a model for universities in other parts of the globe. This is not said in boast.

It is simply that the imperatives that have molded the American university are at work around the world.

Each nation, as it has become influential, has tended to develop the leading intellectual institutions of its world—Greece, the Italian cities, France, Spain, England, Germany, and now the United States. The great universities have developed in the great periods of the great political entities of history. Today, more than ever, education is inextricably involved in the quality of a nation. It has been estimated that over the last thirty years nearly half of our national growth can be explained by the greater education of our people and by better technology, which is also largely a product of the educational system.[2]

So many of the hopes and fears of the American people are now related to our educational system and particularly to our universities—the hope for longer life, for getting into outer space, for a higher standard of living; our fears of Russian or Chinese supremacy, of the bomb and annihilation, of individual loss of purpose in the changing world. For all these reasons and others, the university has become a prime instrument of national purpose. This is new. This is the essence of the transformation now engulfing our universities.

The knowledge industry. Basic to this transformation is the growth of the "knowledge industry," which is coming to permeate government and business and to draw into it more and more people raised to higher and higher levels of skill. The production, distribution, and consumption of "knowledge" in all its forms is said to account for 29 percent of gross national product, according to Fritz Machlup's calculations; and "knowledge production" is growing at about twice the rate of the rest of the economy.[3] Knowledge has certainly never in history been so central to the conduct of an entire society. What the railroads did for the second half of the last century and the automobile for the first half of this century may be done for the second half of this century by the knowledge industry: that is, to serve as the focal point for national growth. And the university is at the center of the knowledge process.

The university historically has been growing in concentric circles. It started with philosophy in Greece, and a library—the first great one—at Alexandria. It spread to the ancient professions, and then to science. It permeated agriculture and now industry. Originally it served the elites of society, then the middle class as well, and now it includes the children of all, regardless of social and economic background.

Spatially the modern university often reflects its history, with the library and the humanities and social sciences at the center of the campus, extending out to the professional schools and scientific laboratories, and surrounded by industry, inter-

spersed with residence halls, apartments, and board-
ing houses. An almost ideal location for a modern
university is to be sandwiched between a middle-
class district on its way to becoming a slum and an
ultramodern industrial park—so that the students
may live in the one and the faculty consult in the
other. M.I.T. finds itself happily ensconced between
the decaying sections of Cambridge and Technology
Square.

Universities have become "bait" to be dangled
in front of industry, with drawing power greater
than low taxes or cheap labor. Route 128 around
Boston and the great developing industrial com-
plexes in the San Francisco Bay Area and Southern
California reflect the universities in these areas. The
Gilpatric report for the Department of Defense explained that 41 percent of defense contracts for
research in the fiscal year 1961 were concentrated
in California, 12 percent in New York, and 6 percent
in Massachusetts, for a total of nearly 60 percent,
in part because these were also "centers of learning."[4] Sterling Forest outside New York City seeks
to attract industry by location next to a new university campus.[5] In California, new industrial laboratories were located next to two new university
campuses before the first building was built on
either of these campuses.

Sometimes industry will reach into a university
laboratory to extract the newest ideas almost before
they are born. Instead of waiting outside the gates,

agents are working the corridors. They also work the placement offices. And the university, in turn, reaches into industry, as through the Stanford Research Institute.

The new connection of the university with the rise and fall of industrial areas has brought about an inter-university and interregional competition unmatched in history except by the universities and their *Länder* in nineteenth-century Germany. Texas and Pittsburgh seek to imitate what California and Boston have known; so also do Iowa, Seattle, and nearly all the rest. A vast campaign is on to see that the university center of each industrial complex shall not be "second best."

It is often through new academic specialties and through athletics that the universities seeking to rise in the academic hierarchy can most quickly and easily attract national attention—and also by hiring great and visible academic stars. The mark of a university "on the make" is a mad scramble for football stars and professorial luminaries. The former do little studying and the latter little teaching, and so they form a neat combination of muscle and intellect.

The university and segments of industry are becoming more alike. As the university becomes tied into the world of work, the professor—at least in the natural and some of the social sciences—takes on the characteristics of an entrepreneur. Industry, with its scientists and technicians, learns an uncomfortable bit about academic freedom and the handling of intellectual personnel. The two worlds are merging physically and psychologically.

The rise of Ideopolis. University centers have a tendency to coalesce. Allan Nevins has put it this way: "Observers of higher education can now foresee the inexorable emergence of an entirely new landscape. It will no longer show us a nation dotted by high academic peaks with lesser hills between; it will be a landscape dominated by mountain ranges." [6] The highest peaks of the future will rise from the highest plateaus.

One such plateau runs from Boston to Washington. At the universities and laboratories situated along this range are found 46 percent of the American Nobel Prize winners in the sciences and 40 percent of the members of the National Academy of Sciences. A second range with its peaks runs along the California coast. C. P. Snow has written: "And now the scientific achievement of the United States is moving at a rate we all ought to marvel at. Think of the astonishing constellation of talent, particularly in the physical sciences, all down the California coast, from Berkeley and Stanford to Pasadena and Los Angeles. There is nothing like that concentration of talent anywhere in the world. It sometimes surprises Europeans to realize how much of the pure science of the entire West is being carried out in the United States. Curiously enough, it often surprises Americans too. At a guess, the figure is something like 80 percent, and might easily be higher." [7]

The California mountain range has 36 percent of the Nobel laureates in science and 20 percent of the members of the National Academy of Sciences. The Big Ten and Chicago constitute a third range of academic peaks, with 10 percent of the Nobel laureates and 14 percent of the members of the National Academy of Sciences. These three groupings of universities—the East Coast, California, and the Big Ten and Chicago—currently produce over three quarters of the doctorates conferred in the United States. Another range may be in the process of development in the Texas-Louisiana area.

This concentration of talent partly follows history —the location of the older private and public universities. Partly it follows industrial strengths and population centers. But it also has its own logic. No one university can cover all specialties, or cover them well enough so that there is a sufficient cluster of close intellectual colleagues. The scholar dislikes intellectual isolation and good scholars tend to swarm together. These swarms are extraordinarily productive environments. No library can be complete; nor any graduate curriculum. Some laboratories, to be well used, must be used by more than one university. Thus the Big Ten and Chicago, through their Committee on Institutional Cooperation, are merging their library resources, creating a "common market" for graduate students, diversifying their research laboratories on a common-use basis, and parceling out foreign language specializations. Something similar is happening in the University of California system, and between Berkeley and Stanford. Harvard and M.I.T., Princeton and Pennsylvania, among others, run joint research enterprises.

These clustering universities, in turn, have clustering around them scientifically oriented industrial and governmental enterprises. To match the drawing power of the great metropolis, there now arrives the new Ideopolis. The isolated mountain can no longer dominate the landscape; the constellation is greater than the single star and adds to the brightness of the sky.

There are other possible patterns for development. France and Russia have not made their universities so central to the life of society. They have segregated their research institutes to a substantial degree and established separate institutions for much of their technical training. Also, both have set up their universities on a regional basis with one university having a monopoly in the region. Both France and Russia, however, are now making their universities more central mechanisms, and Paris and Moscow, in particular, are the dominating institutions. Nevertheless, their basic pattern is quite different from the American, and, I think, not as productive.

With these national, industrial, and academic

pulls upon them, universities need to be quickly responsive to opportunities, readily adaptable to change. Yet they are basically conservative institutions. Jacques Barzun in his *House of Intellect* presents this "House" from an inward looking and idealistic point of view, as one opposed to the "corruption" of science, to modern art, to foundations with their interdisciplinary projects, and so forth, regretting that the "House" is no longer "a company apart." [8] However, the "City of Intellect" of the modern university also must look outward and to reality; it cannot be "a company apart." This conflict between internal and external dynamics has always been a difficult one for universities but never so intense as at present when the imperatives of change press so unmercifully against the necessities of internal harmony.

CONSERVATIVE INSTITUTIONS—DYNAMIC ENVIRONMENT

There are two great clichés about the university. One pictures it as a radical institution, when in fact it is most conservative in its institutional conduct. The other pictures it as autonomous, a cloister, when the historical fact is that it has always responded, but seldom so quickly as today, to the desires and demands of external groups—sometimes for love, sometimes for gain, increasingly willingly, and, in some cases, too eagerly. The external view is that the university is radical; the internal reality is that it is conservative. The internal illusion is that it is a law unto itself; the external reality is that it is governed by history.

The university's gate of Janus leads inward as well as outward, and inside the gate the social landscape changes remarkably. When one looks inward toward the "ivory tower," he sees a different "looking-glass land." Here, to get somewhere, you must run twice as slowly. This is as it must be. The university, as an institution, needs to create an environment that gives to its faculty members:

a sense of stability—they should not fear constant change that distracts them from their work;

a sense of security—they should not need to worry about the attacks against them from outside the gate;

a sense of continuity—they should not be concerned that their work and the structure of their lives will be greatly disrupted;

a sense of equity—they should not be suspicious that others are being treated better than they are.

Inventiveness should be left to the individual faculty member within the protection and solidity of the surrounding institutional structure. Galileo within the conservative institution of Padua in his day, Erasmus at Oxford and Freiburg, Newton at Cambridge helped start the enormous metamorphosis from which the modern world emerged. But their institutions, as institutions, were stolidly changeless.

The faculty guild. "Nothing should ever be done for

the first time" was the wry conclusion of F. M. Cornford from his vantage point as a classicist at Cambridge University at the turn of the century when Cambridge was stirring with responses to the modern world. He added that "Nothing is ever done until every one is convinced that it ought to be done, and has been convinced for so long that it is now time to do something else."[9] John Stuart Mill had looked upon the British universities of his day as largely unrelated to the progress of national life. Harold Laski, a century after Mill, felt that Oxford and Cambridge operated under a form of "syndicalism," which he considered the antithesis of the social usefulness he sought, and that they were only partly saved by being shaken up by royal commissions every thirty or forty years. Flexner referred to universities generally as "institutions usually regarded as conservative, frequently even as strongholds of reaction," and added that "institutions as such tend for quite obvious reasons to lag behind the life which they express and further."[10]

With reference to the American scene, Frederick Rudolph in his recent authoritative study of American colleges and universities concluded that "Resistance to fundamental reform was ingrained in the American collegiate and university tradition, as over three hundred years of history demonstrated. . . . Except on rare occasions, the historic policy of the American college and university [was]: drift, reluctant accommodation, belated recognition that while no one was looking, change had in fact taken place."[11] Nevitt Sanford, after a study of more contemporary focus, observed that there have been few innovations at all and even fewer "initiated by college or university faculties"; when a movement for reform has come, "it is the collective faculty who usually seem to be dragging their feet."[12]

There is a kind of "guild mentality" in the academic profession, as in many others. The guild was isolationist toward society, devoted to producer as against consumer sovereignty, and committed more to guild rules than to quick adaptation to popular demand. The guild was egalitarian, full of senatorial courtesy, selective of its own members. It was also a "sort of club" as Snow has characterized the colleges of Cambridge and Oxford,[13] and an "oligarchy of senior professors" as Ashby has noted about these same institutions.[14] In Germany, the faculty was more a class structure than a guild—a class structure intimately tied into the class structure of the surrounding society, hierarchical rather than fraternal.

The self-contained guild idea is still an attractive ideal. One recent call to faculty members is to "close our gates," become "masters within our walls," assume a "posture of offence" against the surrounding society.[15] Yet, except in a few situations, the faculty guild has never been a fully self-governing guild in reality, and almost never a company of "free agents,"[16] much as it might like to believe itself one. However, the guild idea, the "Republic of Scholars," is often and understandably the faculty member's vision of "pie-in-the-sky."

Some of history has swirled past the "guild"; some has disrupted it; some has transformed it; some has swept it entirely away. Much of the Renaissance occurred completely outside the university. The university was generally allied against the Reformation, although bitter fights were fought within many universities, and in some the reformers emerged triumphant. The industrial, democratic, and scientific revolutions have gradually moved in on the universities and changed them almost beyond recognition. Some revolutions, like the French and Russian, placed the "guild" fully under state control, although it has regained some of its ancient rights in France. In all of these intellectual and social revolutions, the university, as an institution, was initially more a "stronghold of reaction" than a revolutionary force, although the ideas of its individual members have often been a stimulus to change.

Eric Ashby has said that policy should "seep gradually upward" within the guild.[17] Sometimes it has. In Oxford and Cambridge, research of extraordinary quality developed when the guild was still in control and still devoted to the classics. But, generally, change, when it has come, has been initiated or at least assisted from outside the gates, as the case of England today so decisively demonstrates. The educational revolution now going on there comes from the outside and above, and finds its greatest proponents in the Labor Party.

The individual faculty member, and particularly the political liberal on the faculty, is often torn between the "guild" and the "socialist" views of the university. The guild view stands for self-determination, and for resistance against the administration and the trustees; the socialist view, for service to society which the administration and the trustees often represent. The guild view is elitist toward the external environment, conservative toward internal change, conformist in relation to the opinion of colleagues. The socialist view is democratic toward society, radical toward change, and nonconformist. And the political liberal is drawn toward both views. Here is a paradox. Few instituitions are so conservative as the universities about their own affairs while their members are so liberal about the affairs of others; and sometimes the most liberal faculty member in one context is the most conservative in another. The natural radical, within the context of the guild, is radically conservative. The faculty member who gets arrested as a "freedom rider" in the South is a flaming supporter of unanimous prior faculty consent to any change whatsoever on his campus in the North. The door to the faculty club leads both out and in.

Change is a traumatic experience for an academic community, as for others. The Yale faculty in 1828 rejected in theory, while proving in practice, that colleges "by being immovably moored to the same station . . . serve only to measure the rapid current of improvement which is passing by them." [18] In a very real sense, the faculty is the university—its most productive element, its source of distinction. And faculty members are properly partners in the enterprise with areas reserved for their exclusive control. Yet when change comes it is rarely at the instigation of this group of partners as a collective body. The group is more likely to accept or reject or comment, than to devise and propose. The group serves a purpose as a balance wheel—resisting some things that should be resisted, insisting on more thorough discussion of some things that should be more thoroughly discussed, delaying some developments where delay gives time to adjust more gracefully to the inevitable. All this yields a greater sense of order and stability.

Institutional changes are coming, however, in areas under faculty control or influence. Some of the needed revisions will be troublesome. In many places, curricula and calendars will need to be restudied; undergraduate teaching renovated; faculty concepts of equality of treatment revised; mechanization of some elements of instruction installed; some fields of study (like biology) revolutionized. These changes will come in the face of much faculty hesitation and even some resistance. At least two changes, however, will have faculty support. One will be directed toward overcoming the fractionalization of the intellectual world, and the other will call for procedures devised to make administration more personal, including faculty administration.

The faculty world seems to sense a loss of unity—intellectual and communal unity. In large measure this can be attributed to "the overwhelming predominance of things that are new over things that are old" and to what Robert Oppenheimer calls "a thinning of common knowledge." [19] Knowledge is now in so many bits and pieces and administration so distant that faculty members are increasingly figures in a "lonely crowd," intellectually and institutionally. It is a sad commentary on the "community of masters" when its elements come together in interchange only when they coalesce feverishly over a grievance about some episode related to a change of the calendar or a parking fee.

Quite fortunately, however, there is a kind of senatorial courtesy within the collective faculty about changes desired by a single member, or a few. Changes initiated from the outside, as in the development of the federal grant university, which also have their internal supporters, are especially easy to accomplish. The individual faculty member seeking something new has, in turn, often found his greatest encouragement and leverage coming from the outside; the individual scholar is the inventor, the outside agency the force for innovation. The inventing faculty member almost instinctively knows that internal change will come more easily if he obtains the external support of a foundation or a federal agency. These outside-to-inside and inside-to-outside alliances have been great sources of progress.

Much change also takes place largely outside collective faculty purview, outside the "veto groups" of the academic community—in the new department or institute, the new project, the new campus. The institute, in particular, has been as much the vehicle of innovation in recent years as the department has been the vault of tradition. Change comes more through spawning the new than reforming the old.

When change does come, it may be by the slow process of persuasion, or by subversion as through the inside-outside alliance, or by evasion as in the new enterprise, or by external decision. The academic community, regardless of the particular process involved, is more changed than changing; change is more unplanned than planned.

"*Remembrance of things past.*" If the collective faculties represent the present, the collective alumni represent the past—as much the best of the past as the faculty the best of the present. The alumni are oriented toward their own undergraduate days. There seems to be a rising sense of alumni concern as the rate of change rises. Generally it is over the preservation of an emphasis on teaching as against research; of the beauty of the old campus as against the asphalt and concrete and glass of the recent "improvements"; of the quality of remembered undergraduate life in its totality; of the old admission requirements which let the old grads get in; of athletic teams that never lost a game; of the spirit of the "halls of ivy" as against the technological materialism of the federal grant university; of the integrity of the old alma mater against the blandishments from Washington. The older and the smaller and the more private and the more distinguished the university, the greater the intensity of these concerns.

If the alumni are concerned, the undergraduate students are restless. Recent changes in the American university have done them little good—lower teaching loads for the faculty, larger classes, the use of substitute teachers for the regular faculty, the choice of faculty members based on research accomplishments rather than instructional capacity, the fragmentation of knowledge into endless subdivisions. There is an incipient revolt of undergraduate students against the faculty; the revolt that used to be against the faculty *in loco parentis* is now against the faculty *in absentia*. The students find themselves under a blanket of impersonal rules for admissions, for scholarships, for examinations, for degrees. It is interesting to watch how a faculty intent on few rules for itself can fashion such a plethora of them for the students. The students also want to be treated as distinct individuals.

If the faculty looks on itself as a guild, the undergraduate students are coming to look upon themselves more as a "class"; some may even feel like a "lumpen proletariat." Lack of faculty concern for teaching, endless rules and requirements, and impersonality are the inciting causes. A few of the "nonconformists" have another kind of revolt in mind. They seek, instead, to turn the university, on the Latin American or Japanese models, into a fortress from which they can sally forth with impunity to make their attacks on society.

If federal grants for research brought a major revolution, then the resultant student sense of neglect may bring a minor counterrevolt, although the target of the revolt is a most elusive one.

The big state universities are most vulnerable to charges of neglect of students. The private universities, tied more to tradition, to student tuition, to alumni support, to smaller size, have generally far better preserved their devotion to undergraduate life.

In inter-university competition, the distribution of the ablest students, as shown by the statistics on scholarship winners, is a telling point. A university's share of the ablest students is an important element in its ranking: how attractive is its educational program to the students most entitled to make a choice?

Student pressures for better undergraduate instruction may be supplemented by the complaints of parents, who think their children are being sacrificed on the altar of research. Also, the public at large, whose attention has been riveted on the elementary and secondary schools as the "population bulge" has affected them, may now turn its attention increasingly to the university level when the "bulge" reaches there. Generally the public is more interested in quality of instruction than in quantity of research. The spotlight which the universities have helped turn on the teaching of others at lower levels may now be turned on their own.

External imperatives. The truly major changes in university life have been initiated from the outside, by such forces as Napoleon in France, ministers of education in Germany, royal commissions and the University Grants Committee in Great Britain, the Communist Party in Russia, the emperor at the time of the Restoration in Japan, the lay university governing boards and the federal Congress in the United States—and also, in the United States, by the foundations. The foundations, quickly responsive to needs and possibilities, have been the main instruments, for example, in the reform of medical education, the introduction of interdisciplinary studies, the involvement of universities in world affairs. As catalysts, their influence has been enormous. The new developments might have been undertaken within the universities themselves, but they were not.

Prospective changes can be identified, in part, by the interests of the external initiators—trustees, state governments, foundations, industry, the federal government. What are the current concerns? There are:

problems related to costs, identified particularly by Beardsley Ruml—faculty-student ratios, fuller utilization of the calendar, excessive numbers of courses, mechanization of instruction; [20]

problems related to accommodation of the vast numbers of young people already knocking on the doors;

problems related to public service—cultural programs, urban extension, advice to state and federal legislators and agencies;

problems related to the supply of trained personnel for industry and the public, particularly engineers, scientists, and doctors;

questions about the quality and availability of research, particularly the establishment of additional university research centers;

problems related to the exploitation of new discoveries, particularly in the biological sciences and spreading out into the health sciences and agriculture.

Additionally there is a general public concern with "morality" on the campus; with the so-called beatniks, with the young radicals, with cheating, and with sex. There is also a deep concern about how far, and how fast, research discoveries may change the lives of everyone. These "moral" concerns fill the incoming mailbox of the administrator.

The external origin of most changes raises very

grave problems: how to identify the "good" and the
"bad," and how to embrace the good and resist the
bad. There is also a problem of timing—how to
adjust not too rapidly and not too slowly. And there
are the problems of how to change the content of
the university without changing its essential forms;
of how to reconcile the conservatism of the collective
faculty with the radical function of the total institution as carried out primarily by the individual
faculty members. These obligations to select the
good and reject the bad, to pace the rate of change,
and to discover the methods of change that will do
least damage to traditional processes fall primarily
on the reluctant shoulders of the administrator. And
as Cornford remarked: "You think (do you not?)
that you have only to state a reasonable case, and
people must listen to reason and act upon it at once.
It is just this conviction that makes you so un-
pleasant." [21]

Today, changes are occurring quite rapidly and
spontaneously. In addition, inter-university rivalry
has become so intense that the rate of acceptance of
change has been accelerated. The current problem
is not so much that the university does not fully
control the direction of its own development—it
seldom has—but rather that it must make what are
judged to be essential adjustments so often and so
quickly, like an amoeba in an unfriendly environment. This has added to the strains placed on the
internal structure of the institution. At the same

time, however, the current rate of growth in numbers helps to relieve these strains, for a period of growth necessarily involves considerable flexibility. Still, the major test of the modern American university is how wisely and how quickly it adjusts to the important new possibilities. The great universities of the future will be those which have adjusted rapidly and effectively.

THE NEW FACES OF CHANGE

The universities are currently facing three great areas of related adjustments: growth, shifting academic emphases, and involvement in the life of society. The direction of adjustment in each of these areas is reasonably clear; the detailed arrangements and the timing are not.

1. *Growth.* The number of university and college students in the United States will almost double during the 1960's. This addition of three million will duplicate in one decade the growth of the three centuries since Harvard was founded. The proportion of graduate students will rise considerably, and there are already 25,000 postdoctoral students.

Existing campuses are being enlarged and many new ones founded. This will be the greatest period of campus renovation and establishment in American history. A particularly large number of junior colleges will be formed as the junior college movement becomes nationwide.

New centers of graduate strength are emerging, and a network of alliances is being formed among the old and the new centers in the competition to ˙offer the greatest total combination of resources.

To accommodate the great increase in enrollments, many calendars are being rearranged, particularly in state-supported institutions, to permit more nearly year-round use of physical facilities. Students will be able to accelerate their work if they wish, and generally students will come and go with less reference to their "class"; more of them will drop in and drop out as suits their particular schedules and needs.

There will be some further mechanization of instruction (television, language laboratories, programmed learning) to improve quality and to save faculty time for other endeavors, including more individual work with students. The sciences will almost eagerly embrace these aids to learning. The foreign language departments will be rather reluctant, because these devices can threaten their structure of faculty employment and the recruitment and utilization of graduate students.

Because of the competition for faculty members, salaries will continue to rise; fringe benefits of all sorts will be devised to tie professors to a particular campus. In addition to competition among universities, there is also intensified competition with industry and government. This competition has obvious advantages in raising faculty income but it has its negative aspects. As the market becomes more active, internal equity will be injured, for some disciplines are much more in demand in the market than others. Teaching loads will be competitively reduced, sometimes to zero, although more teachers are needed and students are complaining about lack of attention. The identification of the professor with his university will be generally loosened—he will become more a member of a free-floating profession. The rules regarding how much time a professor can spend away from his university assignments and those affecting the sources of his income within the university will continue to be in great flux.

This current phenomenon of rising salaries and benefits, however, may be of relatively short duration, lasting, perhaps, for the remainder of this decade. Faculty salaries have been catching up with incomes in other professions after an historical lag. By 1970, also, the personnel deficit of today may be turning into the surplus of tomorrow as all the new Ph.D.'s roll into the market. A new plateau of compensation may be reached in the 1970's. But in the long run, it is common labor more than uncommon talent that is rising in its comparative monetary evaluation, as the educational process uncovers more talent and depletes the ranks of those willing to do common labor.

2. *Shifting academic emphases.* Knowledge is exploding along with population. There is also an ex-

plosion in the need for certain skills. The university
is responding to all these explosions.

The vastly increased needs for engineers, scientists, and doctors will draw great resources to these
areas of the university. Also, some new professions
are being born. Others are becoming more formally
professional, for example, business administration
and social work. The university becomes the chief
port of entry for these professions. In fact, a profession gains its identity by *making* the university the
port of entry. This creates new roles for education;
but it is also part of the process of freezing the
structure of the occupational pyramid and assuring
that the well-behaved do advance, even if the gen-
iuses do not. The university is used as an egg-
candling device; and it is, perhaps, a better one than
any other that can be devised, but the process takes
some of the adventure out of occupational survival,
and does for some professions what the closed shop
has done for some unions. The life of the universities
for a thousand years has been tied into the recognized professions in the surrounding society, and
the universities will continue to respond as new
professions arise.

The fastest-growing intellectual field today is
biology. Here there is a veritable revolution where
the doctrine of evolution once reigned supreme. To
the classifying efforts of the past are being added
the new analytical methods of the present, often

drawn from chemistry and physics. There are levels of complexity to be explored in all living structures. The "code of life" can now be read; soon it will be understood, and soon after that, used. It is an intellectual discovery of unique and staggering proportions. The secrets of the atom, much as they have changed and are changing human activity on this planet, may hold no greater significance than the secrets still hidden in the genetic code. If the first half of the twentieth century may be said to have belonged to the physical sciences, the second half may well belong to the biological. Resources within the universities will be poured into the new biology and into the resulting new medicine and agriculture, well supported though medicine and agriculture already are.

Another field ready to bloom is that of the creative arts, hitherto the ugly ducklings or Cinderellas of the academic world. America is bursting with creativity in painting, music, literature, the theater with a vigor equaled in few other parts of the world today. Italy, France, Spain, Germany, Russia, England, the Low Countries have had great periods of cultural flowering. America is having one now. In the arts the universities have been more hospitable to the historian and the critic than to the creator; he has found his havens elsewhere. Yet it is the creativity of science that has given science its prestige in the university. Perhaps creativity will do the same again for the humanities, though there may be less new to create than has recently been true in science and the tests of value are far less precise. A very important role remains for the historian of past ages of creativity and for the critic of the current productions. But the universities need to find ways also to accommodate pure creative effort if they are to have places on stage as well as in the wings and in the audience in the great drama of cultural growth now playing on the American stage.

These possibilities for expansion—in the training of engineers, scientists, doctors, and the newer professionals, in biology, and in the creative arts, among various others—raise again the problem of balance. As James Bryant Conant has noted, the Western world has had for a thousand years a continuing problem of "keeping a balance between the advancement of knowledge, professional education, general education, and the demands of student life." [22]

But the balance is always changing; this is the unbalancing reality. The balance is not equal treatment, the provision of equal time in some mechanical and eternal way between teaching and research, or between the humanities and science. The dynamics of balance did not give equal treatment to the available scientist in Padua in 1300 when Giotto was painting his chapel, or to the available artist in Padua in 1600 when Galileo was lecturing from his crude platform. Balance cannot be determined on the scales by blind justice, field versus field and activity versus activity.

The essence of balance is to match support with the intellectual creativity of subject fields; with the need for skills of the highest level; with the kinds of expert service that society currently most requires. None of these measures is constant. Balance requires, therefore, a shifting set of judgments which relates facilities and attention to the possibilities inherent in each field, each skill, each activity at that moment of time in that environment, yet preserves for all fields their essential integrity. To know balance is to know the potential creativity, the potential productivity, the potential contribution of each competing activity in an unfolding pattern of time and an evolving landscape of environment. To know balance is to know more than anyone can ever know in advance. But decisions must nevertheless be made and time will tell how well. The only certainly wrong decision is that the balance of today must be preserved for tomorrow. Where will the world's work and the university's work best be done? The answer to that question is the true definition of balance.

3. *Involvement in the life of society.* Knowledge is now central to society. It is wanted, even demanded, by more people and more institutions than ever before. The university as producer, wholesaler and retailer of knowledge cannot escape service. Knowledge, today, is for everybody's sake.

The campus and society are undergoing a somewhat reluctant and cautious merger, already well advanced. M.I.T. is at least as much related to industry and government as Iowa State ever was to agriculture. Extension work is really becoming "life-long learning." Harvard today has four postgraduate doctors in its medical school for every one still working for his degree; so also for many other skills including business. Television makes it possible for extension to reach into literally every home; the boundaries of the university are stretched to embrace all of society. The student becomes alumnus and the alumnus continues as student; the graduate enters the outside world and the public enters the classroom and the laboratory. Knowledge has the terrifying potential of becoming popular, opening a Pandora's box.

The campus becomes a center for cultural life; it has a ready-made audience in its students and faculty and it has the physical facilities. Persons attracted by the performing and visual arts and the lectures come to live around the campus—also assorted crackpots. As the downtown area in some cities decays, the campus takes its place as the cultural center of the community. A new dimension has been added to the land grant idea of service.

The New Deal took professors to Washington from many campuses, the New Frontier from more than just one. In Wisconsin before World War I, the campus and the state house in Madison were exceptionally close. Today the campus is being drawn to the city hall and the state capital as never before. The politicians need new ideas to meet the new problems; the agencies need expert advice on how to handle the old. The professor can supply both. Keynes concluded his *General Theory* as follows: ". . . the ideas of economists and political philosophers, both when they are right and when they are wrong, are more powerful than is commonly understood. Indeed the world is ruled by little else. Practical men, who believe themselves to be quite exempt from any intellectual influences, are usually the slaves of some defunct economist. Madmen in authority, who hear voices in the air, are distilling their frenzy from some academic scribbler of a few years back. I am sure that the power of vested interests is vastly exaggerated compared with the gradual encroachment of ideas." [23] As, for example, the ideas of Keynes.

The university must range itself on the side of intelligent solutions to sometimes unintelligent questions. These questions more and more arise from abroad as well as at home; and the quality of the answers has been made all the more crucial in a world swept by Communist and nationalist revolutions.

There are those who fear the further involvement of the university in the life of society. They fear that the university will lose its objectivity and its freedom. But society is more desirous of objectivity and more tolerant of freedom than it used to be. The university can be further ahead of the times and further behind the times, further to the left of the public and further to the right of the public—and still keep its equilibrium—than was ever the case before, although problems in this regard are not yet entirely unknown. There are those who fear that the university will be drawn too far from basic to applied research and from applied research to application itself. But the lines dividing these never have been entirely clear and much new knowledge has been generated at the borders of basic and applied research, and even of applied knowledge and its application.

Growth and shifting emphases and involvement in society all take money; and which universities get it in the largest quantities will help determine which of them excel a decade or two hence. Will federal support be spent according to merit or according to political power? Will private donors continue to do as well as they recently have for those universities that have done well already? Will the states find new sources of revenue or will their expenditures be held under a lid of no new taxes? The answers to these questions will help predict the standings on the next rating scale of universities.

However this turns out, the scene of American higher education will continue to be marked by great variety, and this is one of its great strengths. The large and the small, the private and the public, the general and the specialized all add their share to over-all excellence. The total system is extraordinarily flexible, decentralized, competitive—and productive. The new can be tried, the old tested with considerable skill and alacrity. Pluralism in higher education matches the pluralistic American society. The multiversity, in particular, is the child of middle-class pluralism; it relates to so much of the variety of the surrounding society and is thus so varied internally.

The general test of higher education is not how much is done poorly, and some is; rather it is how much is done superbly, and a great deal is, to the nation's great benefit. Although it has been said that the best universities in America have been caught in a "stalemate of success," [24] there is no stalemate; there is some success.

CHANGES STILL TO COME

There has been some success, but there are some problems still to be fully faced; and they are problems of consequence.

One is the improvement of undergraduate instruction in the university. It will require the solution of many sub-problems: how to give adequate recognition to the teaching skill as well as to the research performance of the faculty; how to create a curriculum that serves the needs of the student as well as the research interests of the teacher; how to prepare the generalist as well as the specialist in an age of specialization looking for better generalizations; how to treat the individual student as a unique human being in the mass student body; how to make the university seem smaller even as it grows larger; how to establish a range of contact between faculty and students broader than the one-way route across the lectern or through the television screen; how to raise educational policy again to the forefront of faculty concerns. Increasingly, aiso, the better institutions will need to keep in mind that many of their undergraduate students will be going on to graduate school, and therefore that they need individual attention as pre-graduate students.

Another major task is to create a more unified intellectual world. We need to make contact between the two, the three, the many cultures; to open channels of intelligent conversation across the disciplines and divisions; to close the gap between C. P. Snow's "Luddites" and scientists;[25] to answer fragmentation with general theories and sensitivities. Even philosophy, which once was the hub of the intellectual universe, is now itself fragmented into such diverse specialties as mathematics and semantics. However, the physical sciences are drawing together as new discoveries create more basic general theories; the biological sciences may be pulled together in the process now going on; the social sciences might be unified around the study of organizations and the relations of individuals to and within them. Chemistry and social psychology may come to be central focalizing fields. As knowledge is drawn together, if in fact it is, a faculty may again become a community of masters; but "a sense of the unity . . . of all knowledge" [26] is still a very long way off.

A third problem is to relate administration more directly to individual faculty and students in the massive institution. We need to decentralize below the campus level to the operating agencies; to make the collective faculty a more vital, dynamic, progressive force as it now is only at the departmental level; to bridge the growing chasm between the department that does the teaching and the institute that does the research, with the faculty member torn between; to make the old departments and divisions more compatible with the new divisions of knowledge; to make it possible for an institution to see itself in totality rather than just piecemeal and in the sweep of history rather than just at a moment of time; to bring an understanding of both internal and external realities to all those intimately related to the process, so that there may be greater understanding; to see to it that administration serves and stimulates rather than rules the institution, that it be expendable when necessary and flexible all the time; to assure that the university can do better what it does best; to solve the whole range of governmental problems within the university.

Additionally, there is the urgent issue of how to preserve a margin for excellence in a populist society, when more and more of the money is being spent on behalf of all of the people. The great university is of necessity elitist—the elite of merit—but it operates in an environment dedicated to an egalitarian philosophy. How may the contribution of the elite be made clear to the egalitarians, and how may an aristocracy of intellect justify itself to a democracy of all men? It was equality of opportunity, not equality *per se,* that animated the founding fathers and the progress of the American system; but the forces of populist equality have never been silent, the battle between Jeffersonianism and Jacksonianism never finally settled.

If there are to be new departures, they are most likely to come on the campuses of those old, private universities which have prided themselves on control of their own destiny, and on the totally new campuses of the state universities in America and the new public universities in Britain. The university for the twenty-first century is more likely to emerge from these environments than from any others. Out of the pride of the old and the vacuum of the new may come the means to make undergraduate life more exciting, intellectual discourse more meaningful, administration more human. And perhaps there will arise a more dynamic demonstration of how excellence makes democracy more vital and its survival more assured. Then the universities may rise to "the heights of the times" and overcome "their inspirational poverty." [27]

George Beadle, president of the University of Chicago, once implied that the very large American university (but not his own) might be like the dinosaur which "became extinct because he grew larger and larger and then sacrificed the evolutionary flexibility he needed to meet changing conditions";[28] its body became too large for its brain. David Riesman has spoken of the leading American universities as "directionless . . . as far as major innovations are concerned";[29] they have run out of foreign models to imitate; they have lost their "ferment." The fact is that they are not directionless; they have been moving in clear directions and with considerable speed; there has been no "stalemate." But these directions have not been set as much by the university's visions of its destiny as by the external environment, including the federal government, the foundations, the surrounding and sometimes engulfing industry.

The university has been embraced and led down the garden path by its environmental suitors; it has been so attractive and so accommodating; who could resist it and why would it, in turn, want to resist?

But the really new problems of today and tomorrow may lend themselves less to solutions by external authority; they may be inherently problems for internal resolution. The university may now again need to find out whether it has a brain as well as a body.

THE CITIES OF INTELLECT

We have been speaking of the City of Intellect as a university city with its satellite suburbs. The City of Intellect may be viewed in a broader context, encompassing all the intellectual resources of a society, and the even broader perspective of the force of intellect as the central force of a society— its soul. Will it be the salvation of our society?

The organized intellect is a great machine that has gained extraordinary momentum since the Greeks got it going 2500 years ago. It turns out its countless new pieces of knowledge but with little thought for their consequences—their impact on the environment—like a new insecticide. Its attention to problems quite naturally does not always relate primarily to their importance but often, instead, to the possibility of their solution. Thus the problems of rising population and rising levels of destructive capacity move along without study commensurate with their inherent significance. Does this machine have within it the "seeds of its own destruction"? Or can it develop an over-all rationality? As Lee DuBridge of Cal Tech has said: "Scientists and engineers do worry about the consequences of their works. But neither they nor anyone else has discovered how to avoid or even to predict these consequences." [30]

The process cannot be stopped. The results cannot be foreseen. It remains to adapt. And here the social sciences and humanities may find their particular roles in helping to define the good as well as the true and to add wisdom to truth. It may not be the conflict of cultures that is so crucial but rather the rate at which each culture moves forward. Can the intellect come to handle all the problems it creates in the course of solving other problems? Can the university help solve the growing war between the future and the past? Can the span of intellectual comprehension be widened spatially and temporally?

Intellect has also become an instrument of national purpose, a component part of the "military-industrial complex." Our Western City of Intellect finds its counterpart or counterparts in the East. In the war of the ideological worlds, a great deal depends on the use of this instrument. Knowledge is durable. It it also transferable. Knowledge costs a great deal to produce, less to reproduce. Thus it only pays to produce knowledge if through production it can be put into use better and faster. The Communist City of Intellect has been a planned community. It grows only in certain directions and in certain ways. This allows concentration of effort but limits growth and recognition except in restricted segments of the intellectual world. This City flourishes in science and in military might but lags in the humanities and the social sciences. Whole areas that would be covered by a really modern City of Intellect are largely unpopulated.

The two Cities of Intellect are not only sources of weapons— they also form a potential bridge between their two societies. Knowledge is universal. Its creators generally prefer freedom. To the extent the Eastern City of Intellect grows and makes contact with the Western, it almost inevitably changes its own society. Here a certain type of society really may carry the "seeds of its own destruction." It either competes and changes, or it loses some of its over-all power of competition.

Marx saw technology as the major force in history; but intellect creates technology and the logic of intellect's development may be quite different from the unraveling of the "mode of production" as Marx visualized it. History has seldom, if ever, proved a theorist to be so incorrect and at the same time so influential as Marx. The wave of the future may more nearly be middle-class democracy,[31] with all its freedoms, through its better use of intellect in all intellect's many dimensions, than the "dictatorship of the proletariat" (which, in fact, is the dictatorship of the single party). But it has not yet been proved conclusively whether intellect can preserve and even create the culture of freedom, in which it best flourishes, more effectively than technology, under Communist leadership, can be used to bolster dictatorship.

The intellect, and the university as its most happy home, can have great potential roles to play in the reconciliation of the war between the future and the past, and the solution—one way or the other— of the war between the ideological giants who now rend the world with their struggles. Certain it is, however, that the reconciliation of the future and the past can only be made more elusive in the context of an ideological struggle where survival is almost the sole essence of rational behavior. The two problems compound each other's effects.

At the outset I quoted Cardinal Newman on his "Idea of a University," reflecting the beautiful ivory tower of Oxford as it once was. It seems appropriate to conclude with Alfred North Whitehead's prophetic words in 1916 on the place of intellect: "In the conditions of modern life, the rule is absolute: the race which does not value trained intelligence is doomed. Not all your heroism, not all your social charm, not all your wit, not all your victories on land or sea, can move back the finger of fate. Today we maintain ourselves. Tomorrow science will have moved forward yet one more step, and there will be no appeal from the judgment which will be pronounced on the uneducated."[32]

These are the uses of the university.

POSTSCRIPT—1972

Much has happened to higher education and to the United States since these lectures were written in the early spring of 1963 and presented at Harvard toward the end of April of that year. That was a conservative period in higher education—not in the sense that nothing was happening, for a great deal was, but in the sense that what was happening was mostly adding quantity and quality to what was already being done. The directions then generally appeared to be quite clear to most: to accommodate the tidal wave of students and to expand and improve research capabilities, particularly in science. Yet the early signs of a new period of reform, and even of revolt and counter-revolt, were already evident, as these lectures then noted.

Cardinal Newman wrote in 1852 about the classical British university when it was already beginning to be conquered by the German model, and conquered even in Britain. Abraham Flexner portrayed in 1930 the ideal of the German research university after it had long given way to the American version of greater service orientation in the United States and as it was about to give way to the Nazi-dominated university in Germany. These Godkin lectures, in turn, described the American model just before it met its greatest challenges after a century of development and growth.

One may wonder whether a model comes into somewhat clearer sight only as it exits from the stage of history and makes way for some new institutional participant with a quite different character. Whether or not a slow exit is what is now happening to the American model, I do not think that anyone can yet be sure. Will 1870 to 1970 have been the century of the rise and the beginning of the decline of the American university? Or, after a pause for a time of troubles, will it gain new strength and rise to greater heights? I leave this simply as a question, for this "Postscript—1972" is concerned, not with what has happened since 1963 or what may happen in the future, but, rather, with how I now wish I had written these lectures *in 1963*. To begin with, however, I should like to reaffirm my conviction about the continuing validity of certain of the central themes.

THEMES REAFFIRMED

Many, and even most, of the themes of 1963 have been accented by intervening events—a few in a rather spectacular fashion:

1. The "new centrality" of the university is now even more widely recognized, not only because the university adds to knowledge and extends the uses of knowledge in an age of ever newer knowledge (page vii of this book), but also because political and cultural changes, in part, originate within it. The university has even been said recently to be the "paramount institution" in "post-industrial society."[1]

2. The modern university was presented as a "new type of institution"—and new largely because of the new centrality of knowledge—with "a whole series of communities" within it rather than being a "single community" as it once had been and as it was customarily still viewed (pp. 2, 1). The university was seen as both more central to society and also changed within itself. As the many internal fissions have emerged in recent years, it has become increasingly apparent that the university "means many things to . . . many different people," and that neither all of these many things nor all of these different people are fully unified with each other (p. 8). What was called in 1963 a "multiversity" has, in fact, on occasion, become a Tower of Babel partially falling apart rather than being held loosely together.

3. Consensus and tolerance were set forth as essential to keeping intact the "whole uneasy balance" of the multiversity (p. 18). I called it an

"inconsistent" institution that could survive best only as the "moderates" kept control. "Extremists" could turn the situation quickly into "war." So many possible points of conflict could be exploited (pp. 20, 39).

The loss of consensus and of tolerance over the past decade has indeed led to many campus wars as the potential points of conflict, previously partially obscured by a history of unbroken peace, became actual points of conflict—students versus faculty, humanists versus scientists, younger versus older faculty members, and so forth. Below the placid surface of 1963 lurked the largely unsuspected strains. A narrow barrier of tolerance stood between peace and war—not much separated them from each other—and, when tolerance was gone, what had been unbroken peace became intermittent warfare. The "delicate balance" was delicate indeed (p. 34).

4. The organized faculty was presented as having a "guild mentality" marked by resistance to change in its essential internal affairs except as a slow collegial unanimity emerged (p. 97). The university has been shocked by many external and internal crises over the past few years, but it is remarkable not how much has changed but how little has changed on so many campuses in those areas that are under faculty control and where the faculty feels strongly about its control.[2] The more the environment has changed, the more the organized fac-

ulty has remained the same. It has been the greatest single point of institutional conservatism in recent times, as it has been historically. Little that it has held dear and that it could control has been allowed to change.

5. The period of 1870 to 1920 was presented as the era of the president, when "giants" led the way in dramatic changes, and the period since 1920 as one of "administrators" instead of giants (pp. 34-35). A period of stability in goals and methods, as from 1920 to 1960, tends to be one marked by the rise of academic administrators surrounded by faculty power. The theme was that giants were most likely to emerge in a period of rapid change in goals or methods or both. We are now entering such a period once again, or so it now seems, and some new presidential giants are needed to give leadership to the changes. Virtually all successful major reforms or revolutions in the academic world have come into being and probably will continue to come into being through leadership from the top—or from the outside—through the instrumentality of an Eliot, or a Napoleon.

6. The federal influence from the outside was already being felt in 1963—the "federal grant university" had arrived (p. 46). In retrospect, the two great new forces of the 1960's were the federal government and the protesting students. The federal government emphasized science and research, equality of opportunity, impartiality of treatment

among the races, and the innovative role of the federal agency. Much of what has happened to the campus, both good and evil, in the past decade can be laid at the door of the federal government. For the first time in American history there was a growing sense and an increasing reality of the presence of the federal colossus in higher education. And this reality will never go away again. The federal grant university is now on the way to having added to it the federal grant college, as federal aid and influence permeate all the institutions of higher education and not just a few selected universities alone. University and college presidents now cultivate Washington as avidly as they have cultivated state capitals and the Captains of Industry.

7. "Involvement in the life of society" has grown greatly. The campus has even been drawn to the "city hall," and the predicted "Pandora's box" may well have been opened. How to serve the city, as the rural community has long been served, is now a perplexing problem for many campuses. New pressure groups are insisting that knowledge really be for "everybody's sake." The campus still debates involvement while strong elements in society insist upon it (pp. 114–116).

8. Some of what were then seen as the "changes still to come" are now upon us, often with a vengeance. The "improvement of undergraduate instruction" is now a lively and even abrasive subject on many campuses. The need to create "a more unified

intellectual world" that looks at society broadly, rather than through the eyes of the narrow specialist, has now become the insistent demand of students for relevance. The need "to solve the whole range of governmental problems within the university" is now recognized as the battle over governance. "How to preserve a margin for excellence" in an increasingly egalitarian society has become a most intense issue (pp. 118–121). It takes the form not only of the lesser versus the greater research institutions seeking funds and preferment—the state college against the university—but also, within the elite institutions, of demands by some students and faculty members for open admissions, no course requirements, no grades. The populists are inside as well as outside the gates of the elite institutions, and the current cry for equality of result is replacing the older call for equality of opportunity. Academic reform, governance, demands for equality, in a few swift years, have moved up on the agenda from prospective new business to urgent old business.

9. The "incipient revolt" of students is now a national trauma, viewed recently by the public as the Number 1 or Number 2 social issue (p. 103). In 1963, people were still talking about the apathetic generation, the graduating classes of organization men, the uncommitted students. But apathy quickly turned to activism, organization men to anti-establishmentarians, the uncommitted

to the new radicals. In 1963, the possibility of such a sudden change in the academic weather was only dimly seen when seen at all. There were, however, as I then noted, already the "walking wounded" within the multiversity; some students were beginning to visualize themselves as a "lumpen proletariat"—or, in more modern terminology, as prisoners in the campus ghetto; and a few students wanted even then to make the campus into a "fortress" from which society might be attacked (pp. 43, 104).

The "minor counterrevolt" of undergraduate students against their deteriorating situation that I thought likely in 1963 became, instead, a major revolt even as early as 1964; and the walking wounded were soon found among the faculty and the administrators as well as the students (p. 104). That small cloud, so seldom noticed on the horizon in 1963, quickly materialized into a series of cyclones.

10. The public backlash was already gathering in 1963, even before the great frontlash of the student revolt occurred. There was even then concern with the "beatniks, with the young radicals, with cheating, and with sex." These concerns later were exploited by a California political leader who campaigned with the catchy theme of Treason, Drugs and Sex on the campus. The public was also worried about "how far, and how fast, research discoveries may change the lives of everyone." The uni-

versity was accelerating its racing car named Science, hardly noticing that the public was getting ready to reduce the supply of gas. These several public complaints were already filling the "incoming mailbox of the administrator" in 1963 (p. 106). The mail turned into votes and the votes turned into actions faster than had seemed possible; and more than one state got a governor who attacked higher education.

RECONSIDERATIONS

What might in 1963 have been said better or differently or, perhaps, not at all? I shall set forth four major revisions which I wish I had then been wise enough, or cautious enough, to undertake.

1. The term "multiversity" was used in an effort to make clear that we had a new phenomenon, a new kind of university. The older term of university carried with it the older visions of a unified "community of masters and students" with a single "soul" or purpose (p. 1). There was, however, a new reality and it seemed that it would be helpful to have a new word to carry the image of this new reality; to make the point that Alma Mater was less an integrated and eternal spirit, and more a split and variable personality; to call attention to the fact that what had once been a community was now more like an environment—more like a city, a "city of infinite variety" (p. 41). Thus the

word—"multiversity." It was intended as a descriptive phrase; it has, however, become, on the lips of some, a term of opprobrium.

The word was not really new with me. I later learned that it had been used in an internal faculty report at a midwestern university and by a faculty member at Cornell. It had also been employed by presidents of two of the Big Ten universities[3] and perhaps by others. The word, thus, was in the air, and had several more or less simultaneous authors.

It turned out to be a word that was easily misunderstood. A number of people thought it was "multi-university" in the sense of a multi-campus institution. The multi-campus institution is also a recent phenomenon of great importance—40 percent of all college and university students are now in multi-campus institutions—but it is quite a separate, although somewhat related, development. It should have been clear that the "multiversity" was viewed primarily as a single campus phenomenon since modern Harvard was given as the first illustration of the multi-faceted campus.

What I meant by the word was that the modern university was a "pluralistic" institution—pluralistic in several senses: in having several purposes, not one; in having several centers of power, not one; in serving several clienteles, not one (p. 36). It worshiped no single God; it constituted no single, unified community; it had no discretely defined set of customers. It was marked by many visions of the Good, the True, and the Beautiful, and by many roads to achieve these visions; by power conflicts; by service to many markets and concern for many publics. It might have been called a pluralistic university; or a conglomerate university—making an analogy to business; or, as some Germans now do, the comprehensive university; or a number of other things.[4] What I wanted to do was to mark the contrast with a more nearly single-purpose institution having a more monistic spirit, a more monolithic leadership, and a single clientele—whether the older Oxford concentrating on teaching, run by the faculty, and serving would-be gentlemen or the older Berlin concentrating on research, run by the chair professors, and serving new knowledge.

I wish I had then read William James on the "multiverse."[5] It would have given me a good footnote to employ in lectures given at Harvard and helped me to clarify my ideas. James was talking solely about philosophy. He was contrasting "pluralism" with "monism."

The monistic approach, he said, is to find a single "Absolute." Such absolutes might be (although he did not use them as illustrations) the word of God, or the class struggle of Marx, or the survival of the fittest of Darwin, or the infantile sex of Freud; some absolute that determined everything else, that lent a unity to thought, that posited a community where all the parts were internally related, where there was an organic unity with no independent parts, and that yielded an inherent consistency. James noted that such an absolute was effective in conferring mental peace, a degree of certainty.[6] The absolute (and James was against all absolutes) sought to define what was right and what was wrong in the present, to explain the past, to describe the future. It sought to provide sure standards for making decisions and a clear vision of both past and future events.

The pluralistic approach, by contrast, as James noted, sees several forces at work in more or less eternal conflict, sees everything in "flux," sees a state of indeterminism. There is said to be more free will for the individual, and more dysfunction within and between organizations. Parts of the whole, James said, "may be externally related" rather than only internally related. Thus James spoke of the "multiverse" as a situation where "each part hangs together with its very next neighbors," and where "every part" is "in some possible or mediated connexion with every other part." Thus there was a "strung-along type" of unity or a "contiguity" rather than one central absolute to which every part was tied directly. "Nothing includes everything, or dominates over everything." [7]

This may be taken also as a good description of the multiversity with its strung-along type of unity, with its lack of devotion to any single faith and its lack of concentration on any single function, with a condition of cohesion[8] at best or coexistence at next best or contiguity at least (under internal pressures in recent years, some campuses have moved from a state of cohesion to one of coexistence, or from coexistence to mere contiguity of the constituent elements). The multiversity can be compared, as James compared the multiverse, to a "federal republic" as against a "kingdom," a federal republic where attention should be paid to "each form" by itself, rather than only to "all forms" together.[9]

The multiversity, like the multiverse, has weaknesses: loyalty is not so readily given, conflicts are not so easily settled in terms of absolute principles, borders to confine the extension of efforts are harder to define. By contrast, monistic universities, based on the Bible, or the Koran, or the Communist Manifesto, or the Great Books can test loyalty more precisely, can settle disputes more on principle, can limit their functions more readily. But they also tend to be more static in a dynamic world, more intolerant in a world crying for understanding and accommodation to diversity, more closed to the unorthodox person and idea, more limited in their comprehension of total reality.

To the extent that universities are a generating force for new ideas and for critical commentary on the status quo, they are more likely to fulfill this role where Absolute confronts Absolute, where thesis meets antithesis, where one culture contests another; just as biological generation most often occurs where one ecological environment shades into another, where the sea meets the land. Should the model of the university be based more on productive conflict or on doctrinal unity, on the interaction of disparate entities or on the integration of fully compatible parts? The multiversity is based more on conflict and on interaction; the monistic university more on unity and integration. Monistic universities are more like Plato's hierarchical Republic, and multiversities more nearly correspond to Aristotle's search for the Golden Mean. That ancient controversy, over the closed versus the open society, over rigidity of purpose and hierarchy as against constant adaptation and adjustment, has been going on for a long time in many guises, and so will the controversy between the bitter principled enemies and the reluctant pragmatic supporters of the multiversity.

The multiversity is not one thing but many things along a continuum. J. Douglas Brown sought to establish as a separate type the idea of the "liberal university,"[10] like Princeton, with its greater emphasis on teaching and on the student as a "whole man" and its lesser emphasis on professional schools and public service, with its sense of community through reliance on small size and local residence. I see the differences between Princeton and Harvard, rather, as one of degree—with Princeton toward one end of the continuum and Harvard toward the other with a highly desirable diversity in between.

To help coin a word is not the same thing as creating the institution to which it refers, although some seem to confuse the two processes. The multiversity began when professional schools were originally established, beginning with the medical school at the University of Pennsylvania in 1765; when Harvard created the first departments in 1825 and Jefferson the first separate faculties at Virginia in 1824, as against the earlier single faculty with a single curriculum; when the Morrill Land Grant Act was passed in 1862; when Eliot introduced electives in the 1870's and 1880's; when Harper started an extension service at Chicago in 1892; when the "Wisconsin Idea" was born in the early 1900's; and at many other times and in many other places when and where knowledge was subdivided, new services were added, size accumulated. William Rainey Harper's University of Chicago was being called "Harper's Bazaar" already in the 1890's.

If any group can be said to have sponsored the growth of the multiversity, it has been the faculty—choosing ever narrower specializations, emphasizing research, giving service for love and for money and for both. The spirit of the multiversity sprang particularly from the minds and the hearts of faculty members. Yet some faculty members who avidly seek to live in the multiversity, as their chosen habitat, also love to criticize it unmercifully; it is both their self-selected home and their scorned "inter-section of freeways." [11] Their actions in seeking this habitat, however, belie their words in so severely condemning it.[12] They come to this seemingly contradictory position from both the Left and the Right.

2. I wish I had not used the word "mediator" in describing one of the roles of the president or that I had explained it better—not that it is not a good word but rather that it was so generally misunderstood. "Mediator" to many people apparently means a person who merely carries messages back and forth between the parties, plays no independent leadership role, has no ideas or principles of his own. I had tried to set forth the differences in mediation approaches between seeking a current "compromise" and finding a solution that is "effective" in the long-run, and I clearly preferred the latter. But the word "mediator" to many meant unprincipled compromise, nevertheless (pp. 36–37).

I do not retract the idea that the president almost universally is, in part, a mediator of whichever type. He is and of necessity must be. His performance of this role is inherent in the nature of the multiversity. Leadership of any complex organization or society that permits considerable freedom of opinion and expression to its constituent members and groups involves mediation among the diverse elements. There are mediated connexions between "strung-along elements," as James noted, and the president is the chief mediator of these connexions.[13] More than anyone else he must interpret one group to another, set limits to conflict, referee disputes, work out acceptable solutions. This is a highly important and immensely difficult task. It is one of the highest functions of leadership.

But I wish I had used a different word with different public connotations: political leader, or community leader, or campus statesman, or unifier or peacekeeper, or chief persuader, or crisis manager or agent of integration—anything but mediator. The tone should have been conveyed of active leadership, of statesmanlike solutions, of holding the campus together against internal and external attacks, of keeping the peace as against disruption, of using ideas and principles to bind the ties, of relying on persuasion rather than on force, of seeking consent rather than governing by fiat, of being the guardian of reason in debate, decency in human relations and sanity in action, of meshing together the discordant elements into a productive entity. I wish I had made greater use of a phrase I actually did use as an alternative—the "clerk of the meeting" who both draws forth and contributes to "the sense of the meeting" in the Society of Friends (p. 39).

The reaction to the word mediator startled me, partly because I have a high regard for effective mediators, as the leaders at Yale and at Ann Arbor and at Berkeley the past few years have been—people who can work out solutions to highly charged and infinitely complex situations, who can keep the place open and progressing when so many others want to shut it down. Someone must seek concessions among the many conflicting points of view on a complex campus, must find the workable compromises; otherwise the campus is abandoned to irreconcilable non-negotiable demands on the one side and static resistance on the other; otherwise initiative is left in the hands of the fanatic reformers and the fanatic supporters of the status quo—the proponents at both extremes of no compromise.

But I was also startled at the reaction to the single word "mediator" because I talked about the "mediator-initiator" and stressed the role of the president as initiator of progress, and said that "progress is more important than peace to a university." I also spoke of the president in his role as "gladiator" fighting for "freedom and quality." But among these three roles of leadership—mediator, initiator, gladiator—the one that was remembered most was the first and with a definition of compromiser (pp. 37–39).

I said that "progress is more important than peace" (p. 38). I should also have pointed out that the right kind of progress in the shorter run contributes to peace in the longer run even though that progress may disturb the peace in the shorter run by arousing controversy.

I should have added a fourth presidential role. This is the role of image maker—creating a favorable image of the institution and of himself as the public symbol of the institution. In modern society, with the mass replacement of face-to-face relations by intermediate images, images become crucial. This is particularly true of a large institution with its far-flung publics. Thus the president must be concerned with his own image and the image of his institution (and the two are closely related) for the sake of the continuity and improvement of the institution. An additional reason why the president must now be concerned with his role as image maker is that his critics among the radical students and professors have been so phenomenally successful with their own image making through their dress, their rhetoric, their hair styles, and have projected themselves so spectacularly through TV and newspaper headlines; so also have some political leaders on the reactionary right been successful with their exaggerations and their simplistic slogans. Thus the fighting beret of one president was an image maker's answer to the raised fists of his image making opponents. To fight one image it takes another more effective one, but not necessarily a beret.

But there are dangers in this role, as in each of the other three. The pursuit of image may lead to an undue concern with public credit as against private results—with how things look instead of with how things are, with what shows in the short-run as against what counts in the long-run, with a policy of selective cowardice by the president in saving himself instead of his institution. Each role has its dangers and each role confronts the other: the demands of peace can stand in the way of accepting the strains of progress, an interest in uninterrupted progress can inhibit the undertaking of costly battles for freedom and quality in the short term, and gladiatorial efforts against the external and internal opposition can ruin a carefully built image of universal acceptance and approbation. It is a difficult series of roles to fill simultaneously. And many presidents much of the time do actually choose to be "mostly a mediator" (p. 36).[14]

3. For the sake of some readers I should have put in bold type the phrase in the *Foreword* that "analysis should not be confused with approval or description with defense" (p. v). I was mainly concerned with analysis and description, and not with approval and defense.

There were notes of approval, however. I did refer to the "generally optimistic tone" of the approach and made reference to how "consistently productive" the multiversity was "in the search for new knowledge" and "in serving so many of the segments of an advancing civilization" (pp. v, 45).

A larger number of references were made, nevertheless, to "problems" and to "changes"; and there were some critical comments: on how the university had been "led down the garden path by its environmental suitors" and how it needed "to find out whether it has a brain as well as a body." This was saying, in what I thought was blunt language, that the university better find out which profession it really was following (pp. 100, 118–123).

Yet some people have taken analysis to be approval and description to be defense, and to assume or to claim that every act of every multiversity was both approved and defended in these lectures. Thus I learned how easily some persons who call themselves scholars can turn a descriptive "is" into a prescriptive "should be" and then attack the false "should be."

It was curious how fast the approach sometimes changed from first endorsing my criticisms of the multiversity to then claiming that I had created it on behalf of the military-industrial complex and that it should be brought to a grinding halt. At Berkeley, for example, SLATE—the predecessor group to FSM—in the *Slate Supplement* distributed in September 1964, said "we emphatically agree" with the criticisms made in *The Uses of the University* of the neglectful treatment of undergraduate students; my criticisms were taken as solid proof of the contentions advanced by SLATE. Yet some of these same students were shortly even more emphatically claiming that they disagreed with the book on the grounds that it was a defense of all aspects of the nefarious multiversity. The transition from being quoted as a respected critic to being charged as a kept-apologist was quite abrupt. The same persons leapt from one position to the other as it suited their purposes; and not just students did this. Attitudes changed quickly from agreement to condemnation as external factors intervened.

I discovered too how dangerous it can be to describe as clearly and frankly as one could the inherent nature of a controversial institution. Although description is not defense, it can be dangerous nevertheless. Some people live most happily with their cherished illusions and their comfortable myths, and recoil when the mirror of reality is held before them.[15] In particular, the professor who pictures himself as a radical for all seasons dislikes public mention of his very real conservatism about the affairs of his own faculty. One reaction is to smash the mirror.

Would more precautions have reduced the chance of distortions? I quoted Abraham Flexner's view that universities had become "service stations," and I indicated that he did not approve of "service" activities (p. 5). This was turned by some into my saying that the university was a "service station" and that I did approve. I quoted Fritz Machlup of Princeton on the existence of a "knowledge industry" (p. 87). This phrase was then credited to me, then "industry" was turned into "factory," then the word "knowledge" was dropped, and what started out as Machlup's factual description of the "knowledge industry" became my asserted goal to turn the university into a "factory."

These misuses of quotations from Flexner and Machlup are two of the cruder distortions. But this can be expected when some of the commentators ·are giving political reviews rather than academic reviews, like political trials versus legal trials.[16]

4. I wish that I had written the fourth chapter that I had originally intended. Heavy duties as a university president made this difficult and service on an advisory board appointed that spring by President Kennedy in connection with a major national railroad dispute made it impossible.

That chapter was to treat academic reform in general and more particularly the reforms undertaken on the new campuses of the University of California which were shortly to open—San Diego in 1964, and Irvine and Santa Cruz in 1965.[17] Two of these campuses were being organized on a cluster college basis (San Diego and Santa Cruz), one was planning to try out pass-fail grading (Santa Cruz), another was planning to experiment with having no required courses and allowing each student to choose his own program (Irvine), one was hoping to bridge the Two Worlds of C. P. Snow (San Diego), one was looking for new ways of associating knowledge instead of parceling it out in accordance with the standard disciplinary departments (Irvine); and there were other new departures.

These at the time were the three most experimental university campuses in the United States. Planning on each of them had begun in 1958. The very nature of the planning made the point that the multiversity, as it then existed, was not perfect, was subject to variation and possible improvement. On these new campuses solutions were already being sought in 1958 to problems that were dramatically highlighted beginning with the fall of 1964.

I had hoped in this unwritten chapter to indicate how some of the emerging problems could be solved, how some of the needed changes could best be effectuated. That task was postponed until a later time and then undertaken under other auspices. These lectures would have been more complete and better balanced if the missing fourth chapter had been added in 1963; if more attention had then been given to the proper uses of the university in serving the wellbeing of students on campus and of mankind around the world; if the concluding section had treated with the relation of the university to the eternal search for Utopia.

POSTSCRIPT—1982

Once again, much has happened to higher education and to the United States since these lectures
were written in the early spring of 1963 and even
since the 1972 postscript. To higher education: the
student revolts, affirmative action and the Bakke
case, the Higher Education Amendments of 1972
with vast new sums for student aid, universal access
to higher education instead of the earlier mass access, a turn in the labor market against the college
graduate, increasing middle-class hedonism among
parents and its counterpart of "me-ism" among students, the first impacts of the demographic depression, and much else. To the United States: the loss
of the war in Vietnam, Watergate, the oil crises,
brought on by the Organization of Petroleum Ex-
porting Countries (OPEC), and a series of reces-
sions, the failure of our intervention in Iran, the
reincarnation of the Cold War, the fading of the
American dream of increasing affluence stretching
out to the endless horizon, Reaganomics, and much
else. Yet, and this is the central theme of this postscript, the American research university remains

much the same. The Harvard of 1982 is not all that different from the Harvard of 1963, or the Berkeley of 1982 from that of 1963. Most of the rest of higher education has changed very substantially but, and partly because of this, as I shall note below, not the research university.

This slow change should not be so entirely surprising if one looks even briefly at the long trends of history. Heraclitus said that "nothing endures but change." About the university it might be said, instead, that "everything else changes, but the university mostly endures"—particularly in the United States. About eighty-five institutions in the Western world established by 1520 still exist in recognizable forms, with similar functions and with unbroken histories, including the Catholic church, the Parliaments of the Isle of Man, of Iceland, and of Great Britain, several Swiss cantons, and seventy universities. Kings that rule, feudal lords with vassals, and guilds with monopolies are all gone. These seventy universities, however, are still in the same locations with some of the same buildings, with professors and students doing much the same things, and with governance carried on in much the same ways. There have been many intervening variations on the ancient themes, it is true, but the eternal themes of teaching, scholarship, and service, in one combination or another, continue. Looked at from within, universities have changed enormously in the emphases on their several functions and in their guiding spirits, but looked at from without and comparatively, they are among the least changed of institutions.

How can this be so? Universities still turn out essentially the same products—members of the more ancient professions of theology, teaching, medicine and the law, and scholarship. The universities have not been subject to any major technological change as has industry and agriculture and transportation. The faculty members continue to operate as individual craftsmen. Universities, traditionally, as with the churches, have had a degree of autonomy from political and economic control that is quite remarkable, partly because they have been protected by the upper classes, however constituted, at nearly all times in almost every type of society. They have, on occasion, through what has gone on within them, helped to change the world but have themselves been much less changed than most of the rest of the world.

The last two decades in the United States have been no exception to the general rule that the "attributes" of the university (as Spinoza said of God) "are eternal." There have been revolts and crises in these recent times, but the American university has come out of all this much as it went in. I speak here of the approximately 100 "research universities" in the nation, as defined in the Carnegie Classification, and particularly of the half of this number identified as Research Universities I.[1] The phenomenon to explain is not the changes that have taken place in the universities since about 1960 but the changes that have not taken place, to which I shall turn shortly. Some of the explanations for this paucity of change are these:

1. The research universities are part of a loose system of higher education. The great shift from mass to universal access to higher education was absorbed by the community colleges and by the comprehensive colleges and universities, not by the research universities, and particularly not by the Research Universities I. Total enrollments in the public community colleges alone increased ten times over between 1960 and 1980, from 400,000 to 4,000,000, and the percentage of all enrollments increased from 11 to 35, while the percentage of all enrollments in Research Universities I fell from nearly 20 to under 10 percent. This is the contrary of what happened, for example, in Italy, where massive new enrollments were dumped on the preexisting universities. The elite institutions in the United States remained elite; some became even more elite in their admission standards. The rest of the system absorbed the impacts of this enormous historic development. In the course of doing this, the rest of the system also accommodated all those new lesser professions and occupations that would also have diluted the universities. In particular, the one-time teachers' colleges became comprehensive colleges and universities with a vast added array of occupa-

tionally oriented programs. The community colleges and the comprehensive colleges and universities took on, even eagerly, the impacts of universal access to higher education.

2. The research universities are substantially independent from each other, each making its own adjustments. At the time of the student revolts, for example, some made more concessions to students than others, but each in its own way. Contrast this with the overall legislation on university governance that took place in France, Germany, the Netherlands, Sweden, and elsewhere. The American universities also pulled back from their concessions one at a time, and quietly. This was not so possible in Europe where legislation had been enacted.

3. These research universities have many sources of financial support—federal, state and private; and the federal and the private, in turn, are themselves quite diverse. Decline of one source could be, and usually was, offset by increase in another. The universities in the United Kingdom, under the Department of Education and Science and the Universities Grants Committee, on the contrary, rely mostly on a single source, and when disaster strikes, have no other place to turn, as happened in the early 1980's.

4. Almost regardless of what else is happening, society needs the highest skills and the best new knowledge, and, in the United States, the research university is the chief source of both. And higher and higher premiums are being paid for the highest

skills and the best new knowledge. The role of the research university becomes ever more important.

5. The faculties are substantially in control, and they are most conservative about their own affairs, never more so than when their own affairs are not going too well.

Nevertheless, there have been some changes:

1. Many universities are somewhat larger—some significantly so, including Ohio State, the University of Michigan, Michigan State University, and the University of Minnesota.

2. There has been some shift in the composition of the different categories of research universities (from 1963 to 1979), but not all that much (see Table 1). For example, four new universities entered the list of the top twenty recipients of federal funds for academic science (the University of California at San Diego, the University of California at San Francisco, Pennsylvania State University, and Washington University), and four dropped out at least temporarily (New York University, Ohio State University, the University of Rochester, and the University of Texas); but the other sixteen would have been among the leaders in research activity in 1950, and most of them also in 1920. Twelve of the fourteen original members of the Association of American Universities (established in 1900) are now in the top twenty as defined above. Once a reputation has been established, once a set of policies and academic standards has been set in place, once a

Table 1.   Institutions defined as Research Universities, 1963–1965 and 1976

Institution	1963–1965	1976
University of Alabama	X	
University of Arizona	X	X
University of Arkansas	X	X
Auburn University		X
Boston University	X	X
Brandeis University		X
Brown University	X	X
California Institute of Technology	X	X
University of California, Berkeley	X	X
University of California, Davis		X
University of California, Irvine		X
University of California, Los Angeles	X	X
University of California, San Diego	X	X
Carnegie-Mellon University	X	X
Case-Western Reserve University	X	X
Catholic University of America	X	X
University of Chicago	X	X
University of Cincinnati	X	X
Claremont University Center and Claremont Graduate School		X
Colorado State University	X	X
University of Colorado, Boulder	X	X
Columbia University	X	X
University of Connecticut		X
Cornell University	X	X
University of Denver	X	
Duke University	X	X
Emory University	X	X
Florida State University	X	X
University of Florida	X	X
Fordham University	X	
George Washington University	X	X
Georgetown University	X	X
Georgia Institute of Technology		X

Table 1. *continued*

Institution	1963–1965	1976
University of Georgia	X	X
Harvard University	X	X
University of Hawaii, Manoa		X
Howard University		X
University of Illinois, Urbana	X	X
Indiana State University, Bloomington	X	X
Iowa State University of Science and Technology	X	X
University of Iowa	X	X
Johns Hopkins University	X	X
Kansas State University of Agriculture and Applied Sciences	X	X
University of Kansas	X	X
University of Kentucky	X	X
Louisiana State University and A & M College, Baton Rouge	X	X
University of Maryland, College Park	X	X
Massachusetts Institute of Technology	X	X
University of Massachusetts, Amherst		X
University of Miami		X
Michigan State University	X	X
University of Michigan, Ann Arbor	X	X
University of Minnesota, Minneapolis–St. Paul	X	X
Mississippi State University		X
University of Missouri, Columbia	X	X
University of Nebraska	X	X
University of New Mexico		X
City University of New York Graduate School and University Center		X
New York University	X	X
State University of New York, Buffalo	X	X
State University of New York, Stony Brook	X	X
North Carolina State University, Raleigh	X	X

Table 1.   *continued*

Institution	1963–1965	1976
University of North Carolina, Chapel Hill	X	X
Northwestern University	X	X
University of Notre Dame	X	
Ohio State University	X	X
Oklahoma State University	X	X
University of Oklahoma	X	X
Oregon State University		X
University of Oregon	X	X
Pennsylvania State University	X	X
University of Pennsylvania	X	X
University of Pittsburgh	X	X
Polytechnic Institute of Brooklyn	X	
Princeton University	X	X
Purdue University	X	X
Rensselaer Polytechnic Institute	X	
Rice University	X	
University of Rochester	X	X
Rockefeller University		X
Rutgers, The State University	X	X
St. Louis University		X
University of Southern California	X	X
Stanford University	X	X
Syracuse University	X	X
Temple University	X	X
University of Tennessee, Knoxville	X	X
Texas A & M University	X	X
University of Texas, Austin	X	X
Tufts University		X
Tulane University of Louisiana	X	X
Utah State University		X
University of Utah	X	X
Vanderbilt University	X	X
University of Vermont and State Agricultural College		X

Table 1. *continued*

Institution	1963–1965	1976
Virginia Polytechnic Institute and State University		X
University of Virginia	X	X
Washington State University	X	X
Washington University	X	X
University of Washington	X	X
Wayne State University	X	X
West Virginia University		X
University of Wisconsin, Madison	X	X
Yale University	X	X
Yeshiva University	X	X

Sources: For 1976, Carnegie Council on Policy Studies in Higher Education, *A Classification of Institutions of Higher Education, Revised Edition* (Berkeley, Calif., 1976). For 1963–1965, institutions were defined as research universities on the basis of the criteria of the Carnegie Council's 1976 classification.

sense of pride takes over—they all tend to perpetuate themselves. But there may be some changes by the year 2000 in the top twenty and certainly in the top fifty and the top hundred. Diverse geographical locations will be one explanation for change, leading either to more growth or to more decline in enrollments, which will conduce, in turn, to more chances for new endeavors and improvements in old programs or to the absence of such chances. Another explanation will be the extent to which individual institutions make difficult selective changes in academic programs, building on strengths and eliminating weaknesses, or just act "across-the-board," as is comparatively easy to do. A third explanation will be the comparative strength of their professional schools, which (except for engineering schools) are usually strongest in the private institutions, as these professional areas continue to gain in comparative importance. In particular, there may come to be some new peaks of excellence, if strong and wise academic leadership is asserted, in the South and in the Mountain States where few now exist. All the additions to the list of Research Universities I from 1963 to 1979 (five in total) are in the South and the West.

3. Federal research funds for academic science have been spread more evenly around the country. When *The Uses of the University* was first written, the top twenty universities ("the primary federal grant universities") received 50 percent of federal funds for academic science; today the figure is 40 percent. The top thirty now get 50 percent and the top forty receive 60 percent. This is quite legitimate, since scholarly competence has been spread over more institutions. It is how some of the other 40 or 50 percent of federal funds for academic science is spent that is troublesome, since it is distributed now to over 900 institutions as compared with under 800 in 1963, and often for political reasons. There have been no complaints about this from academic sources as long as there have been sufficient funds to go around, and, in fact, this wider distribution,

however wasteful in results, has been supported as politically necessary to protect the support of the top forty or so institutions. The emphasis has shifted gradually, as I earlier feared it might, from "excellence" toward "balance." This shift may continue to take place.

4. A deficit of Ph.D.s in 1963 has turned to a surplus in 1982. The source of new Ph.D.s has changed substantially from 75 percent from the Research Universities I to 50 percent.

5. Professional fields have grown comparatively in enrollments, particularly engineering, business administration, and medicine, and the "academic" fields have declined proportionately. This means, among many other things, that the universities become more conservative in their politics both among students and faculty.

6. A higher proportion of students are women and minorities.

But none of these is a fundamental change.

FUNDAMENTAL CHANGES ATTEMPTED—AND FAILED

Academic reform. Every American research university in the 1960's and 1970's engaged in one or more academic reforms, most of them in many. The same was true of most liberal arts colleges and most comprehensive colleges and universities, but much less so of community colleges. I speak here of "intended internally originated academic structural change"[2] when I use the words "academic reform."

The two great periods of academic change in American higher education were (1) after the Civil War with the land-grant movement and the modernizing efforts of Eliot at Harvard, White at Cornell, Gilman at Johns Hopkins, and others, and (2) in the 1960's. In between there were minor efforts at change aimed mostly at a return to "general education," as those made under Lowell at Harvard. The 1870's and the 1960's had at least two things in common: a spurt of growth in enrollments that made additions of new faculty and new programs much easier, and new surges forward in national efforts in which higher education could participate.

The national efforts in the 1870's were to industrialize rapidly and to settle the whole continental United States, the latter of which meant new agricultural crops in new areas. Higher education became a source of science and technology, of engineers and farm agents, going far beyond the earlier classical education for the historic professions of teaching, medicine, the law, and the ministry. The national efforts in the 1960's were to advance science and technology after Sputnik and to provide more equality of opportunity for members of lower-income groups and for minorities and for women. Higher education intensified its existing emphasis on science and technology (and this in-

volved few changes), and, within the system as a
whole, moved from mass access to universal access
to higher education and opened up several professional fields to women and minorities. The national
efforts in both the 1870's and 1960's were generally
successful, least so in the area of provision of greater
equality of opportunity in the 1960's, and at both
times higher education played a constructive role.

The internal academic changes that accompa-
nied these forward movements were generally fruitful after the Civil War but generally not in the
1960's. I note this latter fact with sadness.[3] I had
high hopes for academically inspired changes and
participated actively in their promotion, particularly as president of the University of California in
the creation of the Santa Cruz campus (about
which Gerald Grant and David Riesman once
wrote that "no university . . . has achieved a more
vibrant pluralism in the forms of intellectual, social,
and aesthetic experiences for undergraduates",[4])
and as chairman of the Carnegie Commission and
later the Carnegie Council on Higher Education,
which made so many proposals for academic
changes, especially in a report entitled *Less Time,
More Options.*[5] I also watched the failure of the
Tussman and Strawberry College experiments at
Berkeley and, as a member of the governing board
of Swarthmore, the only partially effective efforts to
maintain and restore the honors program at that
college—the great innovation of Frank Aydelotte in

the 1920's. I know of no inventory of intentional academic changes of the 1960's that shows their survival rate,[6] but I would judge that about 90 percent were discontinued or so attenuated as to disappoint their authors; but then their authors, under the prevailing circumstances, often expected too much.

Why? The essential conservatism of faculty members about their own affairs is certainly one reason. This is abetted by the tendency to rely on consensus and on the opinions of the older members of any academic group in making decisions. Also, there are no rewards to the faculty members who seek academic innovation, only the burden of long, drawn out, and often disappointing consultation. Most academic reforms are, in fact, initiated by students, who are notoriously inconstant in their efforts, partly because of their rapid turnover and their responsiveness to current fads, and by administrators, who are usually, except in new endeavors, such as a new campus, restrained by convention and by faculty committees in participating actively in academic affairs. Also, adaptations over past decades and even centuries may well have found the best way of doing things, the tried and true. And, more fundamentally, there often may be no best way, only different ways.[7] Half a dozen ways may be equally effective or ineffective, so there is no strong argument for change. The big research university is particularly impervious to structural changes.

But, I think, there are three more reasons why the

attempted changes of the 1960's largely failed. Many changes at that time in American history attracted faculty members and students who, by their nature—often disaffected and disenchanted as they were with academic and political life—would not let anything work well, particularly somebody else's attempted reforms. Reforms were killed by the customers of reform; reforms were stung to death by the hornets they attracted. The reforms of the 1870's, by contrast, attracted the upwardly mobile and docile children of farmers and immigrants, not the sliders down the meritocratic pyramid of success that had been built up by the 1960's.

Another reason is that the changes of the 1960's moved mostly in directions that faculty members by and large opposed. Such changes often called for more time, often much more time, spent with students, and a broader coverage of subject matters, as in "integrated" programs. The changes of the 1870's moved in ways many faculty members (but by no means all) liked—toward specialized courses, self-governing departments, graduate work, student electives, research.[8] The new faculty members, and particularly the new scientists, were avid supporters, even though the older classicists kicked and screamed all the way.

The changes of the 1870's had a central theme—enhancement of expertise, of science and scholarship. The attempted changes of the 1960's were oriented not toward the advancement of knowledge

but toward improved environments for undergraduate students, usually in ways that cost faculty
members in time and attention and emotion. Faculty members at Santa Cruz often complained of
how time was taken from their research and how
their emotions were drained by contact with students. The changes of the 1870's liberated faculty
members; the changes of the 1960's tied them down
to their offices and to their undergraduate students.
The changes of the 1870's liberated faculty members from *in loco parentis* and those of the 1960's en-
slaved them again. It was the students of the 1960's
who wanted *in loco parentis* in terms of personal attention but hated it in terms of impersonal rules
enforced by the dean of students—the form it had
come to take after the 1870's.

The one most successful academic change advo-
cated by the Carnegie Commission, which coined
the phrase and argued its merits, was the "stop-
out," in the form of readily available leaves of absence for students. "Stop-outs" were troublesome to
registrars and housing supervisors but not to faculty. The academic changes of the 1960's originated
in student bull-sessions and in the minds and hearts
of administrators who listened to students; they
died in the faculty clubs. An exception was the reform at M.I.T. which brought undergraduate students into participation with faculty members on
research projects. This reform originated with faculty members and paralleled faculty interests.

A third reason for the difference between the 1870's and the 1960's was that the national thrusts of the 1870's required fundamental academic changes, specifically the creation of the modern university with its emphasis on research and occupational training. The national thrusts of the 1960's, however, could be accommodated within the existing structures; they did not require fundamental changes. Additionally, presidents, who were the great agents of change, had much more power in the 1870's than in the 1960's, and faculties much less.

Some changes of the 1960's were based not on academic but on political concerns and were forced into practice by student pressure, changes such as programs in Black studies, Native American studies, and Hispanic studies. Faculty members generally never liked them; in fact, barely tolerated them. Born in the passion of student activism, they have mostly withered, or at least wilted, in the silent embrace of faculty committees.

I introduced this section with the phrase "intended internally originated academic structural change" and have suggested that the attempted reform movement was a flame that burned brightly for a while and then flickered out, its extinction mourned by only a few. I count myself among those few. But there were academic changes on a major scale that originated in the marketplace external to educational policy considerations, and these "popular reforms" succeeded where the "telic" reforms failed.[9] These changes consisted of the fundamental shift from liberal to vocational studies,[10] and, within vocational studies, from one field to another—with engineering, for example, going up and down in its attractiveness to students like a yo-yo. Business administration and the paramedical specialties were the great gainers. The composition of instructional effort, measured field by field, must have changed by at least one-third over two decades. This was a revolution of major proportions in what faculty members taught, what students studied, what librarians bought, which departments faded or grew in importance, what kinds of classrooms and laboratories were built, and where they were located on campus. In American higher education, changes influenced by the market are accepted in a way that reforms originating in concerns for educational policy are not. An appropriate emblem for the American college might be the traditional open book, but lying on a sales counter.[11]

The Golden Age of the 1960's and 1970's, because of growth, was a comparatively favorable period for academic idealism; some basic improvements could then have been made, but the opportunities were largely missed.

Reconstitution of the university into a direct agent of social reform. Colleges and universities throughout American history have been looked upon as instruments of social reform. Harvard was founded in part to "advance learning and perpetuate it to Posterity; dreading to leave an illiterate Ministry to the Churches, when our present Ministers shall lie in the Dust."[12] In the 1960's and 1970's there were two major efforts to use the university deliberately to change society.

One such effort was by the federal government to increase equality of opportunity. This was done, in part, by offering grants to college students based upon their comparative ability to pay and, in part, by forcing colleges and universities to change their policies to admit more minorities and women as faculty members. Consequently, many more minorities and women have attended institutions of higher education, but most of them come from the higher income groups. Progress in increasing attendance from low-income groups has been meager (see Table 2). It has been easier to change policies and practices and preferences that make distinctions on the basis of sex and race than on income group. Attendance can be made more possible, but the choice to attend remains voluntary, and academic ability and interest are not equally distributed across income groups.[13]

The hope that many of us had that higher education by 1976 would draw equal proportions of students with high academic ability from all levels of family incomes has been disappointed.[14] This remains a still remote but still achievable goal. And,

Table 2.   Composition of students and faculty in
institutions of higher education, 1960 and late 1970's,
in percentages

	1960	Late 1970's
Women		
Undergraduate enrollment	38.0[a]	51.2 (1979)[b]
Graduate enrollment	29.0[a]	48.9 (1979)[b]
Faculty and other professional staff	22.0[c]	24.8 (1978)[d]
Racial and ethnic groups (includes Black, Asian, and Native American)		
Undergraduate enrollment	6.6[e]	13.0 (1978)[f]
Graduate and professional enrollment	6.1[e]	7.8 (1978)[f]
Faculty	—	8.8 (1977)[g]
Black faculty	3.0[h]	4.4 (1979)[g]
Low-income students		
Students from families in bottom one-fifth of national income distribution	8.7[i]	14.0 (1979)[j]

a. National Center for Education Statistics, *Projections of Education Statistics to 1975–76* (Washington, D.C.: U.S. Government Printing Office, 1966), Tables 11 and 12.

b. National Center for Education Statistics, *Fall Enrollment in Higher Education, 1979* (Washington, D.C.: U.S. Government Printing Office, 1980), Tables 2 and 4.

c. Calculated from National Center for Education Statistics, *Digest of Educational Statistics, 1968* (Washington, D.C.: U.S. Government Printing Office, 1968), Table 100.

d. *Digest of Education Statistics, 1979,* p. 101. Women constituted 25.9 percent of full-time instructional faculty in 1979–80 (National Center for Education Statistics, "Women Faculty Still Lag in Salary and Tenure for the 1979–80 Academic Year," Early Release, NCES 80-342).

e. United States Census of Population, 1960, Subject Reports, *School Enrollment,* Final Report PC(2)-5A.

Table 2. *continued*

f. Calculated from National Center for Education Statistics, *Fall Enrollment in Higher Education, 1978* (Washington, D.C.: U.S. Government Printing Office, 1979), Table 29.

g. "Higher Education Staff Information—EEO-6," Report of the U.S. Equal Employment Opportunity Commission, 1977.

h. Institute for the Study of Educational Policy, *Affirmative Action for Blacks in Higher Education: A Report* (Washington, D.C.: Howard University, 1978), p. 25.

i. U.S. Bureau of the Census. *Current Population Reports,* Series P-20, No. 183, "Characteristics of Students and Their Colleges, October 1966" (Washington, D.C., 1969), Table 2; and *Current Population Reports,* Series P-60, No. 105, "Money Income in 1975 of Families and Persons in the United States" (Washington, D.C., 1977), Table 13.

j. U.S. Bureau of the Census. *Current Population Reports,* Series P-20, No. 346, "Population Characteristics: School Enrollment—Social and Economic Characteristics of Students: October 1978" (Washington, D.C., October 1979), Table 25; and *Current Population Reports,* Series P-60, No. 120, Table 5.

in my judgment, much of the progress that has been made has been because of the new temper of the times and the aroused conscience of the academic community, and little because of direct federal intervention.

All those billions of federal dollars in student aid did more to raise college attendance than to change its composition in terms of source of students by level of family income. It may have had a good political effect, however, by indicating the public's concern for a commitment to equality of opportunity—by creating a situation where lack of attendance was more a matter of choice than of necessity. It brought more money into higher education. It also subsidized middle-income hedonism by reducing financial burdens on middle-income parents.

Progress in participation of minorities and women at the faculty level again has been slow, but faster for women than for minorities. The as-yet-smaller sizes of pools of trained people is one reason, but another is that federal programs got off to a late start, after the massive new hirings of the 1960's were past. Still another reason is the difficulty governmental agencies have in challenging the autonomy of universities and their meritocratic standards—and of course prejudice on campus plays a role.

The second effort to use the university to change society was by students with some faculty support. It sought to use the campus as a staging ground to "reconstitute" society through political discussion, demonstration, and protest. The major targets were racial injustice and the Vietnam war, but also environmental pollution and nuclear power, among others. In no case did the students initiate these issues; they did, however, draw each issue more insistently to national attention. In my judgment, the student use of the colleges and universities was largely ineffective. Blacks quickly rejected the proffered leadership of their movement by the upper-class whites on campus. The federal administration, and particularly President Nixon, adroitly used student protest as one way of temporarily increasing acceptance of continuing the war in Vietnam, by encouraging the backlash of public opinion against the students. And, in any event, students abruptly abandoned their efforts in the summer and fall of 1970. The student effort was divisive on campus and off, and costly in morale internally and in support externally. Students generally have been more effective in getting what they have wished by individually voting with their feet, as they choose what they want and do not want by way of courses, programs, and types of colleges, than by expressing themselves with their voices collectively. I believe that student political effort was not bound inherently to be so ineffective. It was ineffective because of excessive and alienating rhetoric, and the occasional use of force. A more reasoned, persuasive approach might have worked. The student lobbies of the 1970's have, by way of comparison, been effective.

Higher education, however, does reform, or at least change, society indirectly in many ways. New knowledge is one of the great moving forces in our society. The more education that people have, the more liberal their attitudes are on issues such as race, sexual practices, and abortion; the more likely they are to be well informed about public issues and to vote in elections; the more likely they are to take better care of their health, to act prudently as investors, to act effectively as consumers; the more likely they are to accept and to adapt to change.[15] Styles of life are affected. The counter-culture did not originate on campus, but it was avidly embraced there and distributed from there in the writings of faculty members and the actions of students and graduates. The "new breed," as Dan Yankelovich identifies it, is essentially defined by acceptance of the counter-culture and now constitutes, it is said, about half of the American population as against the largely non-college "old breed."[16]

The direct use of the university as an instrument of social reform has had a recent record, depending on source, purpose, and methods, that has ranged from partially effective to counter-productive. The presence of institutions of higher education in society, on the other hand, has many fundamental long-term consequences. The presence of the university carrying out its normal functions changes society fundamentally, but the attempted manipulation of the university, for the sake of specific political reforms, changes the university for the worse more than it changes society for the better.

Changes in governance. I once thought that alternative modes of governance had substantial significance in American higher education. I fought very hard for a system of voluntary advisory coordination when we were setting up the Master Plan in

California in 1960. The differential consequences of
alternative forms of governance has been an assumption of many others as well; witness the many
books and articles on the subject and the many battles fought during the past twenty years. I began
questioning my assumption when a study financed
by the Carnegie Commission on the impacts on performance of different forms of state coordination,
from voluntary to compulsory, showed no significant variations in performance.[17] I would now advance the conclusion that, within the range of alternatives considered in the United States,[18] forms of
governance make some difference but not as much
as often supposed.

There have been many battles over issues of governance in recent years: over federal intervention,
particularly in behalf of affirmative action; over the
creation of a federal department of education,
which the Carnegie Council opposed but which I
now think was not worth the cost of opposition; over
forms of statewide coordination; over the creation of
multi-campus systems and the distribution of authority within them;[19] over the placement of students on committees—but they seldom attend, or
participate erratically if they do; over "participatory democracy" more generally, which I define as
giving each identifiable group not only a voice but
also a veto; over collective bargaining by faculty,
which has done more to generate new rules than to
raise the real income of faculty members.

What has been the result of all these battles won and lost? More formal rules, certainly, but there were always a good many, and all of society is moving that way; more internal and external reports to be made, but, again, this is a universal trend; a lessened sense of attachment within the campus community and of institutional autonomy, but, here again, all of society is becoming more integrated; a more conservative, more cumbersome, more time-consuming system of governance. It is ironic that participatory democracy, with its emphasis that all the "people" should be consulted and all groups have a veto, which was supposed to result in more radical decisions, in more speedy and more responsive actions, has meant, instead, more veto groups, less action, more commitment to the status quo—the status quo is the only solution that cannot be vetoed. Instead of releasing the pent-up energy of the masses, participatory democracy has confirmed the power of special-interest groups to stop changes they do not like; and, it has weakened campus leadership—few administrative heads are now raised above the parapets. Where have the leaders gone? They have gone where they have also gone in corporations, unions, and government. The two most serious consequences of changes in the governance of higher education, I believe, are the last two: participatory democracy and weakened leadership—both negative from the point of view of the continued dynamics of American higher education.

But does it matter? The internal life of higher education goes on much the same: the teaching, the formation of the curriculum, the research, the public service. How could this be? I think there is a good explanation. Most decisions are really made outside the formal system of governance, are made in more informal, less bureaucratic ways. The more visible superstructure of governance is less important than the less visible infrastructure. Most decisions about teaching, about curriculum, about research topics and methods, about amount and form of public service are made by individual faculty members. Most decisions made about majors selected, courses taken, and time spent on study are made by individual students. And intense competition among institutions of higher education, public versus private and public versus public, means that all are seeking optimum solutions; none can afford to lag too far behind. Decisions made in these three ways—by individual faculty members, by individual students, and in response to external competition through market pressures—are the most accepted, the least contested, and considered to be the most legitimate.

Looking only at what is happening to the formal superstructure of governance is like looking only at a part of the whole—important, but not all that decisive. What are faculty members deciding individually? How are students voting with their feet? What does interinstitutional competition compel? These are more essential questions than what form a coordinating council should take or whether or not there should be a federal department of education. This is why several different forms of formal superstructure may not have significantly different impacts on comparative results.

But I would still argue for giving leadership a better chance to exert itself. Most successful new policies in higher education have come from the top. We need to reverse the denigration of leadership. Leadership does matter. It was denigrated by students, by faculty, by trustees in the late 1960's and early 1970's. In the spring of 1969, I was invited to attend a meeting of the Association of American Universities. I had not been to a meeting for two-and-one-half years. I said to the executive secretary that I seemed to know only about half of the nearly fifty presidents who were there. He replied that this was easily explained—anyone who held office by the end of that academic year would be halfway up the seniority list. Presidents were used like Kleenex. The institutions survived, but their leaders did not. Yet in a time of troubles, as then loomed and now looms ahead, leaders are more needed but are harder to get to serve and to keep. To the list of presidential attributes I gave in the original lectures (p. 30), I would now add the ability to withstand the frustrations from all of the checks and balances, and the criticism from all of the more active and vocal participants; that is, the possession of nerves like sewer pipes.

My thesis is that, within the confines of the

changes in the governance of universities considered in the United States, and given the heavy emphasis on individually made decisions by faculty members and students and the active competition among institutions, one specific arrangement in governance versus another has minor implications for what actually happens in a university (although processes may be made more time consuming and more personally disagreeable), with the two exceptions of the arrangements for and the spirit of participatory democracy and the reduced effectiveness of leadership. Many battles have been fought over relatively minor alternatives while less attention has been directed toward these two critical issues. Let me say, however, that this conclusion has been reached after directly observing only about thirty years of history. Over a longer span of time some alternatives that now appear to have about the same impact on actual results (such as whether students sit as members of faculty committees or not) might turn out to have greater significance than I have given them here—for example, at a time of a major crisis.

The massive long-run developments in governance have been from dominance by the board of trustees beginning with 1636, to dominance by the president after 1870, to dominance by the faculty after 1920, to present and greater prospective dominance by the student market.

The three fundamental changes attempted over the past twenty years have largely failed. Academic reform was overwhelmed by faculty conservatism. Efforts to turn the university into a direct instrument for social change were thwarted by institutional autonomy when tried from the outside, and by the inconsistencies between efforts at political assault on society and the continuing conduct of the academic purposes of the campus when tried from within. Changes in formal governance have generally made little difference and, when they did, mostly for the worse. All that effort, all that passion, all that turmoil was mostly for naught, but it was also mostly inevitable given the conditions of the times.

WHAT HAVE WE LEARNED OR RELEARNED?

How strong the modern American university is; how well it fits its environment; how resilient it is to attacks; how little subject it is to fundamental changes; how it can survive and advance in the 1980's and 1990's as it did in the 1960's and 1970's.

How important to the university are its autonomy and its financing from a series of independent sources; how significant that there is no one master but rather a series of fifty states and of many independent private boards.

How protected the university is, surrounded by so many other types of institutions of higher education that shield it from overwhelming numbers of students and from educational duties not compatible with its central functions.

How important are the boards of trustees of American universities to their autonomy and to their dynamics, and how important it is that these boards be composed of individuals devoted to the welfare of their institutions, well informed about their affairs, highly sensitive to the special nature and spirit of academic institutions, and capable of good long-term judgment, even in the midst of severe current pressures.

How conservative the faculty is within its departments and its committees, and how volatile it is en masse under stress, when it may do, and sometimes has done, almost any wild thing; how effective it is individually in intellectual pursuits, yet how it can collectively overreact in more emotional matters. How faculty moods change, as from too optimistic in the 1960's to too pessimistic in the 1970's, and how the universities carry on a much steadier course than these shifting moods would imply.

How volatile the students are in their choices of fields of study, their attachment to political causes and instruments, in their styles of life. I once said in the 1950's as Chancellor at Berkeley that the great administrative problems of the day were sex for the students, athletics for the alumni, and parking for the faculty; but it could better be said now that the problems are, instead, athletics for the students who have gone "straight," sex for the professors with some of whom the counter-culture still finds support, and parking for the alumni as they return for their refresher courses.

How attached are the alumni to the university they once knew; how the conservative alumni are mostly the more loyal and active among the alumni; and how easily they can be aroused by change in a liberal direction, as they have been at Yale, Princeton, and Berkeley.

How strong is the underlying public support for higher education; but how strong are the temporary public reactions to departures from what is expected of higher education in its conduct.

How steady the states are in their support of higher education. Average real state expenditures per full-time student in public institutions remained essentially the same from 1968 to 1977, despite all that was happening in the United States and in higher education.[20] And how unsteady is federal support by purpose, as it shifts from one emphasis to another, and in amount.

How great is the role of aggressive governors for good (Rockefeller in New York) or for ill (Reagan in California), but how governors come and go.

How invulnerable the research university is to enrollment changes in higher education as a whole, since its level of enrollment is largely subject to its own control.

How necessary the American research university is to the advancement of research and the preparation of highly skilled personnel, both in ever greater demand. How central the American research universities have become to worldwide academic life at the highest levels.

How the troubles ahead, particularly demographic depression and budget restrictions, will not greatly affect the research universities, much as they may impinge on other segments of higher education.

How the American research university will be even more essential to American society in 1990 or 2000 than it is today or was in 1960.

How the lessons we have learned from the past will continue to be applicable for the foreseeable future, because the universities change so slowly and so little.

I conclude this postscript as I began the original lectures (p. 9) by saying that the research university in America still has a long way to go.

NOTES

PREFACE, 1982

[1] John F. Hughes, ed., *American Education and the State* (Washington, D.C.: American Council on Education, 1975).

[2] *Three Thousand Futures* (San Francisco: Jossey-Bass, 1980), p. 13.

CHAPTER 1: The Idea of a Multiversity

[1] John Henry Cardinal Newman, *The Idea of a University* (New York: Longmans Green and Co., 1947). The quotations used here are from pp. 129, 91, xxvii, 157.

[2] Francis Bacon, "The Advancement of Learning," *Essays, Advance of Learning, New Atlantis and Other Places* (New York: Odyssey Press, Inc., 1937), pp. 214–215.

[3] Abraham Flexner, *Universities: American English German* (New York: Oxford University Press, 1930). The quotations are from pp. 3, 4, 42, 179, 132, 25, 44–45, 197, 193, 231, 235, 197 (again), 178–179.

[4] Harvard University, *The President's Report, 1961–62*, p. 3.

[5] Hastings Rashdall, *The Universities of Europe in the Middle Ages* (3 vols., 1895, ed. F. M. Powicke and A. B. Emden, Oxford: Clarendon Press, 1936), III, 358.

[6] Benjamin Franklin, *Proposals Relating to the Education of Youth in Pensilvania* (Philadelphia, 1749).

[7] *Reports of the Course of Instruction in Yale College by a Committee of the Corporation and the Academical Faculty* (New Haven, Conn.: Hezekiah Howe, 1828).

[8] Allan Nevins, *The State Universities and Democracy* (Urbana: University of Illinois Press, 1962), p. vi.

[9] John J. Corson, *Governance of Colleges and Universities* (New York: McGraw-Hill, 1960), pp. 175–179.

[10] José Ortega y Gassett, *The Mission of the University* (London: Kegan Paul, Trench, Trubner and Co., Ltd., 1946), p. 56.

[11] McGeorge Bundy, "Of Winds and Windmills: Free Universities and Public Policy," in Charles G. Dobbins, ed., *Higher Education and the Federal Government, Programs and Problems* (Washington, D.C.: American Council on Education, 1963), p. 93.

[12] *General Education in a Free Society*, Report of the Harvard Committee with an Introduction by James Bryant Conant (Cambridge, Mass.: Harvard University Press, 1945).

[13] Richard Hofstadter and Walter P. Metzger, *The Development of Academic Freedom in the United States* (New York: Columbia University Press, 1955), pp. 71, 61.

[14] Thorstein Veblen, *The Higher Learning in America* (Stanford, Calif.: Academic Reprints, 1954), p. 85.

[15] Upton Sinclair, *The Goose-Step: A Study of American Education* (Pasadena: John Regan & Co., 1923), pp. 382–384.

[16] Robert Maynard Hutchins, *Freedom, Education and The Fund: Essays and Addresses, 1946–1956* (New York: Meridian Books, 1956), pp. 167–196.

[17] Harold W. Dodds, *The Academic President—Educator or Caretaker?* (New York: McGraw-Hill, 1962).

[18] Frederick Rudolph, *The American College and University: A History* (New York: Alfred A. Knopf, 1962), p. 492.

[19] James Lewis Morrill, *The Ongoing State University* (Minneapolis: University of Minnesota Press, 1960), p. 48.

[20] John D. Millett, *The Academic Community: An Essay on Organization* (New York: McGraw-Hill, 1962), p. 259.

[21] Henry M. Wriston, *Academic Procession: Reflections of a College President* (New York: Columbia University Press, 1959), p. 172.

[22] Eric Ashby, "The Administrator: Bottleneck or Pump?" *Daedalus*, Spring 1962, pp. 264–278.

[23] Hutchins, pp. 177, 169.

[24] A. Lawrence Lowell, *What a University President Has Learned* (New York: Macmillan, 1938), pp. 12, 19.

[25] Rudolph, p. 291.

[26] James Morris, "Is Oxford Out of This World?" *Horizon*, January 1963, p. 86.

[27] James Bryce, *The American Commonwealth,* new edition (New York: Macmillan, 1914), II, 718-719.

[28] Paul F. Lazarsfeld, "The Sociology of Empirical Social Research," *American Sociological Review,* December 1962, pp. 751-767.

[29] David Riesman, *Constraint and Variety in American Education* (Garden City, N.Y.: Doubleday, 1958), pp. 30-32.

[30] Ernest Earnest, *Academic Procession* (Indianapolis: Bobbs-Merrill, 1953), p. 74.

[31] Rudolph, p. 423.

[32] Eric Ashby, "Self-Government in Modern British Universities," *Science and Freedom,* December 1956, p. 10.

[33] Theodore Caplow and Reece J. McGee, *The Academic Marketplace* (New York: Basic Books, 1958), p. 206.

[34] Millett, p. 224.

[35] Wriston, p. 172.

[36] Nevins, pp. 118-119.

[37] Dodds, p. 43.

[38] W. Max Wise, *They Come For the Best of Reasons—College Students Today* (Washington, D.C.: American Council on Education, 1958).

[39] Burton R. Clark and Martin Trow, *Determinants of College Student Subculture,* unpublished manuscript, Center for the Study of Higher Education, University of California, Berkeley, 1963.

[40] Robert Bendiner, "The Non-Teacher," *Horizon,* September 1962, p. 14.

[41] Merle A. Tuve, "Is Science Too Big for the Scientist?" *Saturday Review,* June 6, 1959, p. 49.

CHAPTER 2: The Realities of the Federal Grant University

[1] Don K. Price, "The Scientific Establishment," *Science,* June 29, 1962.

[2] Some of the principal reports, 1960-1963, are as follows:
American Assembly, *The Federal Government and Higher Education* (Englewood Cliffs, N.J.: Prentice-Hall, 1960).
Homer D. Babbidge, Jr., and Robert M. Rosenzweig, *The*

Federal Interest in Higher Education (New York: McGraw-Hill, 1962).

William G. Bowen, *The Federal Government and Princeton University: A Report on the Effects of Princeton's Involvements with the Federal Government on the Operations of the University* (Princeton University, 1962).

Julius H. Comroe. Jr., ed., *Research and Medical Education* (Evanston, Ill.: Association of American Medical Colleges, 1962).

Charles G. Dobbins, ed., *Higher Education and the Federal Government, Programs and Problems* (Washington, D.C.: American Council on Education, 1963).

Harvard and the Federal Government: A Report to the Faculties and Governing Boards of Harvard University (Harvard University, September 1961).

Charles V. Kidd, *American Universities and Federal Research* (Cambridge, Mass.: The Belknap Press of Harvard University Press, 1959).

J. Kenneth Little, *A Survey of Federal Programs in Higher Education: Summary Describing the Programs, Participating Institutions, and the Effects of the Programs on the Institutions* (Washington, D.C.: Government Printing Office, 1962).

Harold Orlans, *The Effects of Federal Programs on Higher Education: A Study of 36 Universities and Colleges* (Washington, D.C.: Brookings Institution, 1962).

Alice M. Rivlin, *The Role of the Federal Government in Financing Higher Education* (Washington, D.C.: Brookings Institution, 1961).

Glenn T. Seaborg *et al., Scientific Progress, the Universities and the Federal Government: A Statement by the President's Science Advisory Committee,* Nov. 15, 1960.

[3] These fourteen specialized research centers are:

Columbia Radiation Laboratory (Columbia)—Department of Defense.

Applied Physics Laboratory (Johns Hopkins)—Department of the Navy.

Hudson Laboratories (Columbia)—Department of the Navy.

Lincoln Laboratory (M.I.T.)—Department of the Air Force.

Argonne National Laboratory (Chicago)—Atomic Energy Commission.

Cambridge Electron Accelerator (Harvard and M.I.T.)—Atomic Energy Commission.

Lawrence Radiation Laboratory (California)—Atomic Energy Commission.

Los Alamos Scientific Laboratory (California)—Atomic Energy Commission.

Princeton-Pennsylvania Proton Accelerator (Princeton and Pennsylvania)—Atomic Energy Commission.

Princeton Stellerator (Princeton)—Atomic Energy Commission.

Jet Propulsion Laboratory (California Institute of Technology)—National Aeronautics and Space Administration.

Brookhaven National Laboratory (Associated Universities, Inc.)—National Science Foundation.

Kitt Peak Observatory (Association of Universities for Research in Astronomy)—National Science Foundation.

Green Bank Radio Astronomy Observatory (Associated Universities, Inc.)—National Science Foundation and Department of the Air Force.

[4] Sidney Hook, "The Impact of Expanding Research Support on the Universities," in Comroe, ed., pp. 235–237.

[5] Malcolm Moos and Francis E. Rourke, *The Campus and the State* (Baltimore: Johns Hopkins Press, 1959).

[6] See James B. Handler, "An Optimistic View," in Comroe, ed., p. 108: "When asked, they much prefer judgment by a jury in Washington to the risk of judgment by colleagues at home."

[7] Homer D. Babbidge, Jr., and Robert M. Rosenzweig, "The Issues," *The Graduate Journal,* University of Texas, vol. V (1962), Supplement, pp. 62–104.

[8] Dael Wolfle, *America's Resources of Specialized Talent* (New York: Harper, 1954), pp. 190–191, 317–322.

[9] Orlans, p. 173.

[10] Hook, p. 238.

[11] Orlans, p. 134.

[12] J. A. Stratton, "Research and the University," *Chemical and Engineering News,* vol. 31, no. 25 (June 22, 1953), pp. 2582–2583.

[13] Nathan Pusey, "The Carnegie Study," in Dobbins, ed., p. 25.

[14] Don K. Price, *Government and Science* (New York: New York University Press, 1954), p. 96.

[15] Logan Wilson, "A New Dimension," *The Graduate Journal*, University of Texas, vol. V (1962), Supplement, p. 164.

[16] Seaborg *et al.*, as cited in note 2, above. See also in this connection the Report of the President's Science Advisory Committee, *Meeting Manpower Needs in Science and Technology: Graduate Training in Engineering, Mathematics, and Physical Sciences*, Dec. 12, 1962.

[17] Roswell L. Gilpatric, *The Changing Patterns of Defense Procurement*, issued by the Office of the Secretary of Defense, June 19, 1962.

[18] *Circular Letter No. 4*, Association of State Universities and Land-Grant Colleges (Washington, D.C., Feb. 13, 1963).

[19] "The situation appears to call for general aid to U.S. universities patterned somewhat after that provided universities in the United Kingdom by the University Grants Committee. In any event, the question arises of direct subsidy to educational institutions in order to increase the over-all strength of their departments and to provide greater flexibility in their administration." National Science Foundation, *Annual Report, 1960*, p. 16.

Also, Sidney Hook, in Comroe, ed., p. 245, says, "Personally, I see the best solution—not the ideal solution, for there is none —in the system that today obtains in England, where through the University Grants Committee the government makes lump grants to universities that are not earmarked for specific purposes. This system would give a university the necessary autonomy to meet educational needs as it sees them, and permit the deployment of resources at the key points of its educational enterprise."

[20] John Walsh, "Congress: Lag in Science Advice Gives Executive an Advantage," *Science*, vol. 139, no. 3549 (Jan. 4, 1963), p. 27.

[21] *Harvard and the Federal Government*, p. 26.

[22] Basil O'Connor, "Science and Government—The Perilous

Partnership," speech delivered Jan. 16, 1963, at the Third Symposium on Immunopathology, La Jolla, Calif.

²³ President John F. Kennedy, *Message on Education*, Jan. 29, 1963.

²⁴ Orlans, p. 169. It might be noted that the designations "public" and "private" have considerably less meaning for the federal grant universities than they once did for institutions of higher education.

²⁵ Orlans, p. 264.

²⁶ Charles V. Kidd, "The Institute Discussion: Research Emphasis and Research Itself," in Comroe, ed., p. 120.

²⁷ Orlans, p. 180.·

²⁸ Alvin M. Weinberg, "Criteria for Scientific Choice," *Minerva*, Winter 1962.

²⁹ See *Report to the President on Government Contracting for Research and Development*, prepared by the Bureau of the Budget and referred to the Committee on Government Operations, United States Senate, May 17, 1962; and *Operation and Management of Research and Development Facilities and Programs, Analytical and Advisory Services and Technical Supervision of Weapons Systems and Other Programs for the Government, In-House and by Contract*, prepared by a committee under the chairmanship of Helge Holst, treasurer and corporate counsel of Arthur D. Little, Inc., and dated April 17, 1962.

³⁰ See the White House special message, *Improving American Health*, Feb. 7, 1963.

³¹ American Assembly (note 2, above), p. 199.

³² McGeorge Bundy, "Of Winds and Windmills: Free Universities and Public Policy," in Dobbins, ed. (note 2, above), pp. 96–98.

CHAPTER 3: The Future of the City of Intellect

¹ Archibald MacLeish, *The Next Harvard* (Cambridge, Mass.: Harvard University Press, 1941), p. 4.

² Edward F. Denison, *Sources of Economic Growth in the United*

States (New York: Committee for Economic Development, 1962).

[3] Fritz Machlup, *The Production and Distribution of Knowledge in the United States* (Princeton, N.J.: Princeton University Press, 1962), pp. 374, 399.

[4] Roswell L. Gilpatric, *The Changing Patterns of Defense Procurement*, issued by the Office of the Secretary of Defense, June 19, 1962, p. 7.

[5] John Fischer, "The Editor's Easy Chair," *Harper's Magazine*, September 1961, pp. 10–16.

[6] Allan Nevins, *The State Universities and Democracy* (Urbana: University of Illinois Press, 1962), p. 114.

[7] C. P. Snow, 110th anniversary banquet speech, Washington University, St. Louis, Mo., Feb. 23, 1963.

[8] Jacques Barzun, *The House of Intellect* (New York: Harper, 1959).

[9] F. M. Cornford, *Microcosmographia Academica Being a Guide for the Young Academic Politician* (Cambridge, Eng.: Dunster House, 1923), p. 32.

[10] Harold Laski, "The American College President," *Harper's Monthly Magazine*, February 1932, p. 319; Abraham Flexner, *Universities: American English German* (New York: Oxford University Press, 1930), p. 5.

[11] Frederick Rudolph, *The American College and University: A History* (New York: Alfred A. Knopf, 1962), p. 491.

[12] Nevitt Sanford, "Higher Education as a Social Problem," in Sanford, ed., *The American College: A Psychological and Social Interpretation of the Higher Learning* (New York: John Wiley & Sons, 1962), p. 19.

[13] C. P. Snow, *The Masters* (New York: Macmillan, 1951), Appendix, p. 382.

[14] Eric Ashby, "Self-Government in Modern British Universities," *Science and Freedom*, December 1956, p. 10.

[15] Frank Pinner, "The Crisis of the State Universities: Analysis and Remedies," in Sanford, ed., p. 91.

[16] Logan Wilson, *Academic Man* (London: Oxford University Press, 1942), p. 71.

[17] Ashby, p. 5.

[18] *Reports of the Course of Instruction in Yale College by a Committee*

of the Corporation and the Academical Faculty (New Haven, Conn.: Hezekiah Howe, 1828), in *American Journal of Science and Arts,* vol. 15 (January 1829), p. 298.

[19] J. Robert Oppenheimer, "Science and the Human Community," in Charles Frankel, ed., *Issues in University Education* (New York: Harper, 1959), pp. 56, 58.

[20] Beardsley Ruml, *Memo to A College Trustee: A Report on Financial and Structural Problems of the Liberal College* (New York: McGraw-Hill, 1959).

[21] Cornford, p. 4.

[22] James Bryant Conant, *Education in A Divided World* (Cambridge, Mass.: Harvard University Press, 1949), pp. 158, 171.

[23] John Maynard Keynes, *The General Theory* (New York: Harcourt Brace, 1936), p. 383.

[24] David Riesman, *Constraint and Variety in American Education* (Garden City, N.Y.: Doubleday, 1958), p. 33.

[25] C. P. Snow, *The Two Cultures and the Scientific Revolution* (New York: Cambridge University Press, 1959).

[26] Karl Jaspers, *The Idea of the University,* trans. H. A. T. Reiche and H. F. Vanderschmidt (Boston: Beacon Press, 1959), 46.

[27] Sir Walter Moberly, *The Crisis in the University* (London: SCM Press, 1949), p. 20.

[28] George W. Beadle, "The University of X," *Context,* Fall 1961.

[29] Riesman, p. 64.

[30] Lee DuBridge, "The Shape of the Future," *Engineering and Science,* California Institute of Technology, February 1962, p. 13.

[31] Clark Kerr, John T. Dunlop, Frederick H. Harbison, and Charles A. Myers, *Industrialism and Industrial Man* (Cambridge, Mass.: Harvard University Press, 1960).

[32] A. N. Whitehead, *The Aims of Education & Other Essays* (New York: Macmillan, 1929), pp. 22–23.

POSTSCRIPT—1972

[1] Daniel Bell in *Public Interest,* Fall 1968.

[2] Nathan Glazer, *Remembering the Answers* (New York: Basic Books, 1970), p. 215.

[3] ". . . the institution is more a 'multiversity' than a 'university' in the older and simpler sense of the word." James Lewis Morrill, *The Ongoing State University* (Minneapolis: University of Minnesota Press, 1960), Preface (n.p.). Virgil Hancher of the University of Iowa, I understand, had also used the word.

[4] Alexander G. Ruthven, long-time president of the University of Michigan, once wrote that "alma mater" had become a "crowded smorgasbord." *Naturalist in Two Worlds* (Ann Arbor: University of Michigan Press, 1963), p. 91.

[5] William James, *A Pluralistic Universe* (New York: Longmans, Green, and Co., 1909).

[6] James, p. 114.

[7] James, pp. 321, 325.

[8] James A. Perkins sets a higher goal of "coherence" where "all the university's activities advance its capabilities to pursue each of its missions." *The University in Transition* (Princeton: Princeton University Press, 1966), p. 49. A still higher goal might be congruence in the sense of harmony and unity.

[9] James, pp. 321–322, 324.

[10] J. Douglas Brown, *The Liberal University* (New York: McGraw-Hill Book Co., 1969).

[11] Edgar Z. Friedenberg, "L.A. of the Intellect," *New York Review of Books* 1:6 (November 14, 1963), p. 12.

[12] Thus professors from UCLA and London (the most multi-multiversity of them all) can write of the "Clark Kerr monstrosity." James M. Buchanan and Nicos E. Devletoglou, *Academia in Anarchy: An Economic Diagnosis* (New York: Basic Books, 1970), p. 177.

[13] He also wrote, "Compromise and mediation are inseparable from the pluralistic philosophy." *A Pluralistic Universe*, p. 313. In *Pragmatism, A New Name for Some Old Ways of Thinking* (New York: Longmans, Green, and Co., 1907), p. 40, James writes of the "mediating way of thinking."

[14] Ruthven wrote of his years at the University of Michigan that he filled "the role of mediator" and was, of necessity, "continuously in hot water." He said that the president "stands, or should stand, squarely between the staff and the trustees and between the deans of the different schools and colleges." Ruthven, p. 35.

[15] Christopher Jencks and David Riesman wrote about *The Uses of the University* as a "much maligned but marvelously perceptive study" and noted how some faculty members "reacted with horror at the mirror . . . held up to them." *The Academic Revolution* (New York: Doubleday and Co., 1968), p. 17.

[16] For such a "political" review see "Berkeley and the Fate of the Multiversity" by Sheldon Wolin and John Schaar (*The New York Review of Books,* March 11, 1965). See also my reply, "On Berkeley and the Multiversity" (*The New York Review of Books,* April 8, 1965).

[17] Partial contents of this planned chapter later appeared, in somewhat different form, as "Toward the More Perfect University," in *The University in America,* Center for the Study of Democratic Institutions, proceedings of a conference held in Los Angeles in June 1966.

POSTSCRIPT—1982

[1] Carnegie Council on Policy Studies in Higher Education, *A Classification of Institutions of Higher Education,* revised edition (Berkeley: Carnegie Council, 1976).

The most selective of the liberal arts colleges (Liberal Arts I in the Carnegie classification) also changed relatively little. They also were not deluged by students, had substantial institutional autonomy, were under strong faculty control, and received substantial financial support with freedom to spend it as they saw fit. Some of the less selective liberal arts colleges (Liberal Arts II) changed greatly in efforts to survive. The other institutions (mostly doctoral granting universities, state colleges and universities, and community colleges) were in between, not threatened in their survival but subject to absorbing many more students, with less autonomy from state and local control, with less authority lodged in their organized faculties, with more dependence on the current student market, with more responsibility to meet the demands of the many new, and lesser, professions and occupations. The research universities, by contrast, were more under guild control, more tied to less changing older and more elite functions, and less affected by the new occupations and the new student clienteles.

[2] I am choosing my words carefully. I say "intended" in the sense of planned by the institution in advance, as compared with adjustments made in response to political or market pressures, and also in the sense of requiring action by the institution above the level of the individual faculty member or the individual department. I say "internally originated" to contrast with changes externally imposed or influenced. I say "academic" to indicate affecting instruction. I say "structural" to mean doing things in a different way and to exclude changed content in courses which goes on all the time. I say "changes" as a more neutral word than reform, which carries the implication that it is better in some way than what it replaces.

[3] I was much interested in a number of changes which were then attempted. Particularly, I was concerned about giving more attention to undergraduate students in research universities, creating more of a sense of an academic community, reducing the fractionalization of the intellectual world, adding more options for the more diversified students to choose among. Also, I felt that experimentation gave a sense of life and dynamism to the academic endeavor; that it drew forth energy and enthusiasm—as in the Hawthorne experiments in industry; that it served as a check and balance against the old ways of doing things; that it released some faculty and students from their sense of frustration and impotence. I was opposed, however, to changes which reduced academic quality (such as academic credit for experience), which repudiated the value of cognitive learning (such as emphases on affective, "touchy-feely" experiences) and which led to excessive early specialized vocationalism.

[4] Gerald Grant and David Riesman, *The Perpetual Dream: Reform and Experiment in the American College* (Chicago: University of Chicago Press, 1978), p. 296.

[5] Carnegie Commission on Higher Education, *Less Time, More Options* (New York: McGraw-Hill, 1970).

[6] Ann Heiss, *An Inventory of Academic Innovation and Reform* (Berkeley: Carnegie Commission on Higher Education, 1973), discussed innovations adopted in the late 1960's and early

1970's, but at a time too close to their inception to estimate their survival rates. For a description and evaluation of thirteen major curriculum reforms, over half of which are still in existence, see Arthur Levine, *Handbook on Undergraduate Curriculum* (San Francisco: Jossey-Bass, 1978), chapter 13. Levine chose to consider the more permanent of the attempted changes. See also Levine, *Why Innovation Fails* (Albany: State University of New York Press, 1980).

[7] A review of forty years of research on methods of teaching concluded that "no particular method of teaching is measurably to be preferred over another when evaluated by student examination performances." Robert Dubin and Thomas C. Taveggia, *The Teaching-Learning Paradox: A Comparative Analysis of College Teaching Methods* (Eugene, Ore.: Center for the Advanced Study of Educational Administration, 1968), p. 31.

[8] For a detailed discussion of the elements of academic change in the late nineteenth century, see Laurence R. Veysey, *The Emergence of the American University* (Chicago: University of Chicago Press, 1965).

[9] Gerald Grant and David Riesman, *The Perpetual Dream*, pp. 15–18.

[10] The decline of general education was caused both by the changing student market and the indifference of or rejection by the faculty of "general education" courses. Faculties held on to the requirements for the major which they cared about but only to the rhetoric and not to reality of "general education."

[11] Abraham Flexner once wrote that American universities "have thoughtlessly and excessively catered to fleeting, transient, and immediate demands;" *Universities: American, English and German* (New York: Oxford University Press, 1930, 1968), p. 44. This was his central complaint. I, however, take the present situation as a fact, and with some strong arguments for it, as compared with any other system of decision making.

[12] "New England's First Fruits, 1643," in Richard Hofstadter and Wilson Smith, eds., *American Higher Education: A Documentary History* (Chicago: University of Chicago Press, 1961), I, 6.

[13] For a discussion of the effects of ability and socioeconomic status on enrollment rates in four advanced nations, see Roger L. Geiger, "The Limits of Higher Education: A Comparative

Analysis of Factors Affecting Enrollment Levels in Belgium, France, Japan and the United States." Yale Higher Education Research Group Working Paper, YHERG-41, New Haven, Conn., February 1980.

[14] "By 1976, the two-hundredth anniversary of the Declaration of Independence, the Commission proposes: That all economic barriers to educational opportunity be eliminated, thus closing the present probability differentials for college access and completion, and graduate school access and completion, among groups of equal academic ability but unequal family income level." The Carnegie Commission on Higher Education, *A Chance to Learn* (New York: McGraw-Hill, 1970), p. 27.

As much as 15 percent of the high-quality talent that might be expected to go on to college does not now do so, based on the short-fall of students in the top quartile in ability from low- and moderate-income families as compared with the attendance rate of students with similar ability from more affluent families. (National Opinion Research Center, Chicago, "High School and Beyond," a study of 1015 U.S. high schools carried out for the National Center for Education Statistics, 1980.)

[15] Howard R. Bowen, *Investment in Learning* (San Francisco: Jossey-Bass, 1977); F. Thomas Juster et al., *Education, Income, and Human Behavior* (New York: McGraw-Hill, 1975); Stephen B. Withey, *A Degree and What Else?* (New York: McGraw-Hill, 1971). For a summary of some outcomes of higher education, see Charlotte Alhadeff and Margaret S. Gordon, "Supplement E: Higher Education and Human Performance," in Carnegie Council on Policy Studies in Higher Education, *Three Thousand Futures* (San Francisco: Jossey-Bass, 1980).

[16] Daniel Yankelovich, "Work, Values and the New Breed," in Clark Kerr and Jerome Rosow, eds., *Work in America: The Decade Ahead* (New York: Van Nostrand, 1979), p. 10.

[17] See Harry Randall Frost, "A Study of Relationships between Certain Characteristics of Statewide Agencies of Higher Education and Selected Indicators of Higher Education," Diss. University of Colorado, 1978.

[18] The changes undertaken, which have included much more drastic innovations, have certainly had a substantial

impact in some other nations, including Germany, Sweden, Denmark, and the Netherlands.

[19] At the beginning of the seventies, forty percent of all students attended colleges and universities which were parts of multi-campus institutions. Clark Kerr, "Foreword," in Eugene C. Lee and Frank M. Bowen, *The Multicampus University* (New York: McGraw-Hill, 1971), p. xi.

[20] Janet H. Ruyle and Lyman A. Glenny, *State Budgeting for Higher Education: Trends in State Revenue Appropriations from 1968 to 1977* (Berkeley: Center for Studies in Higher Education, University of California, 1978), p. 69.

INDEX